NETWORKING FUNDAMENTALS

by Robert French

THE COMPLETE NETWORKER

by Andrew Hall

www.HandyGuides.net

THE HANDY GUIDE TO NETWORKING

Robert French & Andrew Hall

Copyright © 2002 by Robert French & Andrew Hall

First published in the United Kingdom by Sycamore Publishing (TW) Ltd

Printed in England

Sycamore Publishing (TW) Ltd
The Studio, Hanover Close, 85 Mount Ephraim
Royal Tunbridge Wells, Kent, United Kingdom, TN4 8BU
T: +44(0)1892 511165
F: +44(0)1892 549066
E: publishing@sycamoredesign.co.uk

A HandyGuides Publication

To order additional copies, contact www.HandyGuides.net

The authors may be contacted at the following address:
BNI – Kent
4-5 Upper Bridge Street, Canterbury, Kent
United Kingdom, CT1 2NB
T: +44(0)1227 379000
F: +44(0)1227 478555
E: robert@bni.com
E: andrew@bni.com

Jacket design – Malcolm at Sycamore Design
Text design & production – Natalie at Sycamore Design
Proof reading – Rachel Sellers
Typeset in Akzidenz Grotesk by Sycamore Design
Printed by Pica Press, Tonbridge, Kent, United Kingdom, TN9 1RA

First published: November 2002
Second Edition: February 2003

THE HANDY GUIDE TO NETWORKING

IN PRAISE OF NETWORKING

An invaluable guide to all those who are serious about building their business through Networking

Gillian & Martin Lawson   National Directors, BNI UK

Networking works, wherever you are!
When I started BNI in Sweden 1999, I did wonder if the concept really would fit in our cold and uptight country. Are we different? Now three years later, I look upon more than 35 chapters in Sweden, from Luleå in the very north (snow, reindeer, more snow) to the southern parts of Sweden where we play golf and are fishing all year round. Every chapter seems to work equally well! For me it's all about the fundamentals. People like to refer business to other people they trust and have a relationship with. We are not different. That's why BNI is a success here also!

Gunnar Selheden   National Director, BNI Sweden

Look behind any successful person and you will find a support network of like minded individuals all working towards a common goal. Networking skills like any other skills need to be learned and there is no-one better to learn from than Robert French and Andrew Hall who are both Masters of Networking.

Laura Hurren   Executive Director, BNI London & Birmingham

The example, inspiration and encouragement Andrew & Robert have given me is invaluable. Their knowledge, understanding and guidance helped me open 18 BNI networking groups with over 400 members.

Tony Coxhill   Executive Director, BNI Cheshire

THE HANDY GUIDE TO NETWORKING

CONTENTS

THE HANDY GUIDE TO NETWORKING

Acknowledgements

Our sincere thanks to all of the members and Directors of BNI throughout the world who quite simply have taught us all we know. In particular, we would very much like to thank Ivan Misner, the founder of the BNI, who took the potential that was always there in networking, and turned it into a reality for so many business people around the world.

We would also like to acknowledge the BNI Directors and members who have provided the basis for all of the stories and ideas you will pick up in this guide. It is their dedication and commitment to secure for themselves and their BNI Chapters the greatest possible return from active networking that has made this book possible.

And lastly, Lucinda French - Roberts' daughter, for making sense of the original script and patiently helping to put it together!

Robert French & Andrew Hall

Dedications

I dedicate this work to my daughters, Lucinda and Emma, who inspire me constantly, and to Shereen for her tremendous support

Robert French

To my parents who taught me from the very beginning that "Givers Gain" and to Jihong, for making life complete.

Andrew Hall

THE HANDY GUIDE TO NETWORKING

Foreword

We are not teaching the next generation of business professionals anything about building their business through networking or word-of-mouth marketing! Virtually no academic books on business or marketing focus on this area. Consequently, we are graduating scores of young people with college degrees in business and marketing and not giving them one iota of training in an area that almost all business practitioners agree is one of the most critical to the success of any enterprise.

A structured networking system works by putting you in touch with many other business professionals on a regular basis and in a positive environment. A structured networking program is also personally empowering; it's one of the few things that you, or someone who works for you, can do that directly affects your success.

Why wait for people to walk in your door? Why sit idly, hoping that your existing clients or customers will refer you to others? With a structured networking program, you don't have to wait for the results of your last PR campaign to kick in. Networking gives you control and allows you to take ownership of the development of your business. Such a program has worked for millions of people in all types of businesses and will work for you as well.

Robert French and Andrew Hall have tackled this challenge and have written an excellent two part book that can help anyone become a better networker. I have worked with tens of thousands of business professionals in helping them to develop successful networking programs. I can categorically state that if you follow the ideas outlined in their book, you will develop your networking expertise and enhance your abilities to build a word-of-mouth based business through networking. The Handy Guide to Networking is all about building your business by developing relationships and working with your contacts. Robert and Andrew do a tremendous job of showing you how to do that effectively. I am sure you will learn many important things about networking by reading their book.

Ivan R. Misner, Ph.D.
Founder of BNI
Co-Author, Masters of Networking

Dr. Ivan Misner is the Founder and CEO of Business Network International (BNI), the largest referral marketing organisation in the world.
He has also authored four books on networking and word-of-mouth marketing, including The World's Best Known Marketing Secret and Business by Referral.

PART I

NETWORKING FUNDAMENTALS

by Robert French

www.HandyGuides.net

Chapter One

NETWORKING? NO THANKS!

The function was well marketed, it sounded useful and there would be lots of quality business people there. It was easy to book-in with the well prepared tear-off slip and the price was reasonable. This had to be the best "networking" opportunity with such a hot topic, and well-respected speaker. Surely some business this time?

What went wrong? All that turned out to be true and the new information had some value, but three hours resulted in no new networked business. (see part one, chapter four)

Sound familiar? Of course it does. All business people have at some time or another had this experience. The very mention of networking can conjure negative thoughts, problems with computers, a doubtful business opportunity "sold" by an evangelical friend, – probably using stimulants of some kind, - and business 'networking', which wasted a lot of hours and never yielded a decent return.

In the UK, many business people are a bit coy discussing business, probably a throw back to Victorian times. The classic networking event is the Golf Day. A recent example of this took place in the Home Counties. At breakfast, the rules of the day were laid out for the Networking Golf Event.

1. No business was to be discussed during the first eighteen holes.
2. Lunch at 1.00pm – no business please.
3. Eighteen holes pm – concentrate on the golf and get to know your second partner.
4. Dinner after drinks. No business before or at dinner, but after dinner, feel free to secure those contracts.

Now history relates that one gentleman donated the wine, a particularly good Fleurie, and he was generous to a great extent.

The port was a vintage, and complimented a mature Stilton. Following several "pre-prandials", most participants became mellow to a glorious degree. Conversation revolved around the golf, and inevitably the delights of female company. Business was not discussed.

How could an event like this fail to deliver serious business? In fairness, some useful contacts were established, but business – no! The reasons will be examined in chapter four.

Reticence to discuss business, and even more to actually ASK for it, lies behind the disappointment experienced by eight out of ten British business people.

Another such occasion was organised by a "business club". This organisation had been successful with many subscribers and a small magazine issued every eight weeks, (a good idea).

◄◄

Reticence to ASK lies behind the disappointment

With eighty people expected, and a speaker on Presentation Skills, an interesting evening was on the cards. How could you fail this time?

Everybody signed in and paid their £10. A light buffet was washed down by the odd pint or gin and tonic – well deserved after a hard days work in January.

The speaker was interesting and used audience participation with three volunteers who introduced themselves. Did business deals break out? No! Another disappointing Networking do. The reasons will be examined later.

So... another invitation arrives, and gets filed in the bin. Networking does the "net" bit, but fails to deliver the "work" bit, much desired by so many.

Outstanding Business Available

AWESOME returns are available to companies

Having worked for five years in the "strong" contract end of Networking, the only observation one can make is that AWESOME returns are available to companies small, medium, and large, in all fields.

"What Have I Got To Do?"

Reader, there are dozens of ideas for getting business by word of mouth. Commit to read this book TO THE END, and more business is sure to follow. Invest a little time in education, and choose the best ideas. "Networking? Yes please!"

|◀◀

"Networking?
Yes please!"

History Of Networking And Progress Report On Mankind

On the whole mankind is feeling well satisfied with his dominion over the world. Advances over the last four hundred years have been faster than in the previous five thousand. Mostly it has been for the good.

Let's look at a few areas.

Nutrition

Most nations are well blessed with the ability to support their population – a horrible generalisation, where those that can not, suffer extreme deprivation. Recent trends in the most favoured areas are how to educate the population not to over- consume.

Housing

Slums and squatter camps in third world countries are diminishing, as nations provided secure housing against the elements. Another generalisation, since some countries are still too poor, but by a large extent there has been enormous improvement in the last one hundred years.

Travel

This is an incredible area – freedom to move at speed has never been more available for so many, thanks to affordable air fares. Roads may be congested but are effective.

Communications

This area is probably the single biggest recent influence on human behaviour worldwide. It is astonishing to see people in third world countries with mobile phones, and access to the internet. Although well developed, new technologies will continue to push the barriers of belief with "gizmos" still to come.

This area is having the single greatest impact on humanity, – how we tick, how we work, how we see the future, leisure time, how we see our ability to earn a living, how we balance our spiritual side.

Life Expectancy And Health

In civilised countries, it is amazing to see how sharply life expectancy has increased. Far reaching medical research, stimulated by two world wars, have made mankind come to expect better health, aided by adequate nutrition. Long life is now expected.

What Has All This Got To Do With Networking?

Everything, actually. Here is an extract from "Masters of Networking", a New York Times best-seller in 2001. This extract was part of my contribution, and examines how speedily society has changed.

"In Elham, a village near Canterbury, I recently met a very unusual couple. Betty and Jack, both in their sixties, had never left Elham. They were quite content to stay at home.

I, on the other hand, was visiting my fourth country of the year. Who was living the more unusual lifestyle? I suspect it was Betty and Jack.

But things have changed, of course. Two hundred years ago, most Elhamites, except for the young men who served as soldiers, had never visited even nearby towns. They depended almost entirely on one another for daily necessities, social life, and moral guidance. Their fellow villagers were their reference group. And the reference group's standards of behaviour and belief – set by the village elders – were tough and uncompromising, their enforcement swift and harsh. Though they restricted individual liberty, the rules worked to the benefit of all by keeping citizens civic-minded and the village unified and functional.

⏮

Standards were tough and uncompromising

Betty and Jack are now rare birds, an endangered species. Today we move about freely, settling thousands of miles from our early reference group, the family. We are affluent and mobile; we communicate via long-distance phone calls, faxes and email; we get our information from nationwide and worldwide television networks and the Internet.

At the same time, we are unaccountable, even strangers to our next door neighbours".

It seems impossible that people were so traditional so recently, or that the vast majority have evolved so fast, so recently.

It is obvious that Networking used to be so good, and is now so bad.

Where Are WE Now?

Social dislocation has never been greater. Populations are highly mobile, women account for much of the workforce and much of the work is done better by women than men. This has become a major problem for young, semi-skilled men, who traditionally were required in heavy industry, which is now automated or defunct.

Job opportunities occur anywhere, and often away from the place of origin. Families move frequently, and achieve limited social contact before moving again. Parents get left behind.

⏮

It is obvious that Networking used to be so good, and is now so bad

With good road networks, people choose to live thirty or forty miles from the office. They leave early and return late, to eat with the family and retire. They have limited contact with neighbours.

At the workplace, companies side-by-side on an industrial park keep different hours and rarely coincide – different from the days of Jack and Betty mentioned earlier. The roads are very quiet after 8pm as people "cocoon" – as prophesied by Faith Popcorn. They surf the internet or watch the television – archetypal cave dwellers.

Communication is now often by email, even when the recipient is relatively nearby, or where a telephone call could be made. The email is short, but not sweet.

The need for human contact is growing as modern living disassociates us from each other.

Where Are YOU Now?

Only you can answer. Perhaps you've never checked it out. Let's illustrate.

|◀◀

The need for human contact is growing as modern living disassociates us from each other

1. Do you look at a screen all day?
2. Do you work on your own a lot?
3. Do you start early, commute and finish late?
4. Do you meet lots of people, or not many?
5. Do you spend hours in a vehicle in a jam?
6. Do you run your own business, and lack someone to talk to about sensitive issues?
7. Do you work for someone else and carry a lot of responsibility?
8. Do you have good contacts, or any at all?
9. How much of your business comes from referrals?
10. How much of your business is from loyal customers? (Referred customers tend to become loyal.)
11. Do you refer others?
12. Are you bored with your business?
13. Are you working for someone who does not value you?
14. Do you have a power team – closely related operators who pass business to you, and vice versa?
15. Are you prepared to do some new things to advance?
16. Do you suffer from stress? Many do!

How much of your business comes from referrals?

Previous Experience – Been There, Done That

Most business people have networked sometimes by default. Most have recommended something, a car, a film, a holiday, a friend, a restaurant, a job.

Most have attempted networking – joining a Chamber of Commerce, a business association, other networks, such as Rotary, Lions, Kirwanis, Round Table, Federation of Small Biz, Institute of Directors etc. Some business occasionally comes from all such contacts, quite a bit at times for a hard 'net' worker. Most of us have a preference for all such organisations. I have respect for all of them, they all achieve different things and have a part to play.

In the last five years highly focused Networking has started to make an impact on the business community in the UK, and elsewhere around the world. Business Network International is one such company which originated in California, flourished for a decade in the USA before reaching Canada. It subsequently arrived in the UK via Canada, and now boasts some 7,000 business members across the UK and Ireland.

Members have had all their Networking frustrations resolved by this operation, and have come to take for granted a highly developed system which has yielded good business referred, often to third parties. Other copycat organisations have also arrived. Such as Business Referral Exchange and The Business Network each having their own focus.

Membership of such organisations is usually around £300-£1000 per annum.

For those who have not had the good fortune to find such an organisation, the feeling of "been there, done that", may well be the over-riding experience.

Some years ago, an organisation briefly flourished with lunch-time meetings held on a monthly basis. One such meeting held in a Southern Counties town, boasted ninety participants in the first month. Its tenth meeting could only attract twelve businesses. What happened? It was flawed from the start. Nobody got any worthwhile business. (see part one, chapter four, for what could have been)

Other functions involving lunch normally have a speaker, such as Rotary. They may or may not be exclusive to trade and profession. Generally, business is not the main attraction, and is sometimes discouraged. Participation at such events is difficult to maintain early in the new century, with such time constraints on business people in the UK. The leisurely life style of the fifties and sixties is a distant memory!

Chapter Two

ASSESSMENT

Some useful advice passed down by Napoleon Hill in "Think and Grow Rich" was "start with the end in mind."

The suggestion is to assess what you actually want. Do you want a social group of like-minded business people? It certainly has attractions for today's isolated business operator. It could be a talking shop – nothing wrong with that.

It might be that you want referrals from third parties, engineered by a group you have trained and educated about your needs.

Perhaps you need a reference group? This may be a team of people whom you respect and from whom you seek advice. This could be the Institute of Directors for instance.

Are you looking for a group simply to whom you can sell your products and services? Such groups could be buying and selling organisations.

Stock Taking

Write down all the initiatives you have used so far, and score them out of ten. Did they achieve what you wanted? Remember, value your time, it is an irreplaceable resource! How well did your networking activities yield EXACTLY what you wanted, i.e., a good return on time invested.

Implementing Change

The definition of madness is "to keep doing the same thing, but expect a different outcome".

⏮

If what you did before was not working, then embrace change

Change, therefore, is inevitable, if the desired result is more business through word of mouth recommendation. If what you did before was not working, then embrace change. It is usually invigorating, exciting and rewarding. (Believe me, I had to change 96% of the mix. Being a cave dweller, I came from a position of zero!)

Commit To That Change

Members joining the BNI organisation are warned that BIG business is going to take at least seven to nine months, despite a required weekly input. Real commitment is needed. A new habit takes thirty days to stick, a new technique needs months to bear fruit.

Commitment is a scary word, but most people are committed to their work for probably more than five days a week. Adding a networked dimension is all part of that work – it is part of the marketing strategy.

◄◄

Adding a networked dimension part of the marketing strategy

Research The Market Place

Common sense dictates that all the networking organisations should be researched before deciding which one will suit the individual.

Before that, the reader needs to know that there are different types of networks.

1. Strong Contact

These groups require you to pay an annual membership. They have a tight disciplinary code, and a dynamic approach requiring a regular attendance, with perhaps a weekly or twice weekly frequency. They tend to be the most productive, as the constant exposure is so powerful in focussing on the needs of each member. BNI is one such organisation.

2. Casual Contact

These groups also require a membership fee. They tend to hold monthly meetings. Disciplinary requirements are low, and attendance is optional. Generally speaking, this tends to lead to an activity rate of perhaps 15 - 20% of the membership. On the other hand, they often have large memberships. A good deal of the subscription is used to promote and advertise the organisation. They often have a facilitatory role – advice on aspects of business. Consider the Chamber of Commerce and Institute of Directors in this group.

3. Community Groups

As already mentioned, this would cover Rotary Clubs, Lions, Kirwanis and Round Table. The main focus is for successful business people to make a contribution and impact on sectors of the community requiring assistance. They do a great job.

4. Quasi, Political Or Pressure Groups

Three that stand out in the UK, are The Federation of Small Business, Confederation of Business Industry, and National Farmers' Union. Each provides services to the membership, but acts as a mouth piece for their members. There may be others, forgive the omission if I've missed out your group.

The Effect Of Scale Of Business On Choice

This issue is actually not an issue, rather a perceived one. Is the large-scale operator arrogant? Is the small-scale operator lacking in self belief? Does the small operator buy the big operator's arrogance?

Most organisations are enriched by Networking with companies of all types and scale. Remember the old adage "Every Dud knows a Stud!" Five years of exposure has convinced me that you should never look down on anyone – they may hold the key to your next goal. Most

|◄◄

Five years of exposure has convinced me that you should never look down on anyone

large organisations started small anyway – don't buy the put downs. You never know who knows who!

For smaller companies – a word of advice. Choose who you mix with very carefully. If you wish to expand, seek out the company of those who already have. If you stay with your old contacts, it will severely limit your chances of advancement.

All organisations can benefit from Networking. In the UK, such giants as The Royal Bank of Scotland want to join BNI "chapters". Barclays have many business managers in BNI, as do NatWest Bank. Edward Jones stockbrokers also feature in the groups.

Many "one man bands" have grown through BNI from having a "van and a man" to become well established companies with fifteen or more employees in under two or three years.

⏮

All organisations can benefit from Networking

For large organisations, being involved with small to medium sized companies improves their local profile and provides them with a great contact to local trades which they inevitably need from time to time.

It matters little whether the audience is a business owner or an employee. They probably have different agendas – the business owner wants more business, so does the employee, but the motivation will be one of improved communication, with a bonus of enhanced profit.

Chapter Three

GET GOING

Networking Means Get Working

To be successful, a spiders web of contacts, cross contacts, information handling such as application to business card collection and recording, is required. In short, taking a lot of interest in people you have not yet met.

The second part of "networking" is the "work" part. Simply developing an awareness and attending one or two events will not help.

The serious networker develops a lot of energy around this, and reaps colossal rewards in the shape of contracts and deals with major PLCs and organisations that could be worth millions of pounds. It takes time, but beats most other methods of getting business.

The debutante networker needs to understand that time needs to be allocated to making this work. That time should be seen as part of the marketing strategy not simply as an extra-curricular activity. Whilst networking, you have "clocked-on."

◄◄

Time needs to be allocated to making this work

In the USA, where BNI is eighteen years old, members of some years standing generally spend up to fifteen hours every week with other members. This is not idle chit-chat, but they are fuelling their best channel of new business. In the UK members with several years experience do the same, with great results. In Malaysia, business people have a natural aptitude for networking, and invest time in each other particularly the Chinese community.

At the time of writing BNI is moving into Spain, the first Latin European country. An observation of

Spaniards in both Barcelona and Madrid is that their entire life style is centred around spending time together. With a structured networking system, BNI should be a natural progression as it was for the Malaysians.

Strategy Number One – Join Several Networks

This is spinning the spider's web. The bigger the web, the greater the chance to catch more flies.

BNI always recommends that its new members join the Chamber of Commerce. This is a ready made network, highly informative, well-respected, and usually active. Again, a large number of participants are inactive, but the active members are a useful source of contact. Another benefit is that members tend to be from more established and experienced organisations.

The Institute of Directors is another excellent organisation, with its magnificent club in Pall Mall, London. Membership is more active than other organisations, and tends to include influential people from larger companies. This is clearly an excellent organisation to join, but remember, its main aim is to lobby: politicians directly, Government departments and Regulatory Bodies.

The Federation of Small Business has a great many members. This is a highly effective pressure group which presents its case well, and has the ear of very senior Politicians. In many areas, there are active local branches which put on networking lunches – an excellent medium for making new contacts. Again attendance will be amongst the 25% active membership but that is plenty to be going on with.

The other notable networks are Rotary, Round Table, Lions and Kirwanis. All of these have a charitable ambition, and do an enormous amount of good in a localised way. They tend to have fun and raise money for worthy causes. They are another source of business people with good qualities.

In Kent, England, a small scale printer passed a "referral" at a BNI meeting with a value of £4.5 million to a large corporate institution, which resulted in about £95,000 profit! Business people

◄◄

They are another source of business people with good qualities

at the smaller scale should never feel they have less to offer. Networking really is about who you know. CEOs of large organisations often employ a landscape gardener or roofing contractor. Who else do these tradesmen do jobs for? Other CEOs of course. The old adage holds true "Every Dud knows a Stud!" Small businesses are NOT duds, I hasten to point out. Most large organisations were once small too.

Strategy Number Two – Set Goals

Most businesses set goals, short term, mid term and long term. Short term could be today, this week, this month. Medium term could be anything from six months through eighteen months, to five years depending on the nature of the business.

⏮

I have been stunned at the number of companies who don't really have any idea in this area

During five years in the networking industry, I have been stunned at the number of companies who don't really have any idea in this area.

There are many books on goal setting, and goal achieving. My own personal experience in this area has been outstanding. It took me from a tough existence farming in the UK to owning and running an International company operating in three countries, with an annual turnover of £1 million in four and a half years. I put all that down to having a clearly defined set of goals, which I wrote out nearly every morning at 5am for four years.

It has been interesting introducing this strategy to sceptical friends. One in particular, achieved all five written goals in one year, another outstanding example.

What Goals Do We Need In Networking? Quite A Few Actually!

1. How many new business cards can I acquire this week?
2. How many business cards can I give out?
3. How much business do I intend to get referred to me this week/month?
4. How many functions will I attend this month?
5. How much business can I refer to others?
6. How many people can I speak to at a function?
7. How many people can I introduce to others at a function?
8. How much money will I make from this?

◄◄

How much money will I make from this?

9. How many hours am I going to devote to this enterprise?

10. How many organisations am I joining and when? The great thing about goals is that you can reset them. If you set a goal too tough – reset it in manageable, achievable chunks. "How do you eat an elephant? One mouthful at a time!"

If you achieve them within a time frame – and all goals **must** be, then set the next one.

If you don't set goals, hey, you achieve that too – zilch! Ideally, goals should S-T-R-E-T-C-H you. Little is ever achieved inside the comfort zone.

For those not already doing it, goal setting your entire business is essential. Networking is just the marketing arm of the business. A high level of focus, shared with all those involved with running the business can yield huge improvements with no cost attached. Try it.

Measure The Results

Most people undervalue the contribution Networking makes. There are two reasons – firstly, they have no way of recording or measuring where business comes from, which leads to the second reason – they forget!

BNI is one of the few organisations where the results are meticulously recorded, and comparisons are made. Despite this, some individuals in the organisation still fail to record and evaluate. In these cases, statistics show that they forget 54% of all business referred during a year.

By measuring, a business can react to the information – try harder, reward more, learn more, even celebrate more!

All referrals received and given should be recorded, tracked and evaluated. It is not enough to pass a referral – some effort may be needed to "push it into action", more about that in chapter four.

◄◄

All referrals received and given should be evaluated

As with everything, this all gets easier over time.

Work An Event

Woody Allen was quoted as saying "success is 90% about showing up!" There may be some truth in that, but in networking it really does not hold good. People need to learn to be pro-active, but don't try to knock the world dead in one go – one step at a time.

My personal experience is that I was gut wrenchingly shy. With a background in agriculture, the opportunity to beat this affliction was severely limited, but beat it I did. This was done by acute need and huge enthusiasm. Anxiety still grips me when faced with a large audience of 200-300, but pre-match nerves are okay. The day that goes, there is a danger of "loosing the juice."

What do we mean by "work an event?" Basically, work out your reason for attending. If you value your time, decide what return you would be happy with. There HAS to be a return. Most CEOs are probably worth £400 - £500 per hour. You may actually be better off playing golf, or riding your horse. Relaxation is a deadly serious part of being worth £400 per hour.

The return may be new information, a speaker type of event. Fellow attendees may be of little interest. That would be VERY rare, but possible. The return may be to meet eight new contacts, or to renew acquaintances with business people for a special reason. The return may be to meet a new printer, accountant, solicitor etc who you happen to know will be there. The return may be to find some new contacts to pitch with your goods/service. The return may be to have a beer or gin and tonic with some chums – good enough reason!

If it is to network, then set some goals. Adopt the attitude of being a "host" rather than a guest. Can you relate to the social function where somebody handed round the drinks, canapes, sandwiches, or manned the barbeque? The organisers will have been delighted with the help and the "host" has an easy way to move from group to group, making lots of new contacts, or steering towards the particular group of CEOs, power brokers or whatever.

Some suggestions were made earlier in this chapter, about goals to set at an event. Remember, you must NOT use the event to sell your product or service. In other words, this is the moment to ask questions and be genuinely interested in the answers. Only give the other person a small resume of your business, don't launch into lengthy explanation, or you will lose their

◀◀

Remember, you must NOT use the event to sell your product

interest. You use the event to make a contact, a new friend, get their business card, and make a note on it, – date, where met, interests including outside work, and any comments. Of course, you don't do this in front of them!

Don't look over their shoulder to see if someone more interesting is around. Learn to excuse yourself by introducing them to someone else, then make your getaway! People won't do business with you if they think you are bored by them, just human nature. You need to have a goal of how many new contacts you will make, and make a point of not getting stuck with someone who is not going to advance your cause at all. Remember, you are worth £400 per hour, idle chit-chat costs serious cash.

⏮
Have a goal of how many new contacts you will make

At an event in London recently, a truly excellent graphic designer who was looking for large corporate work, found himself amongst 650 businesses from all over the South East. He missed the opportunity by talking to a chum, both with pints in hand, leaning against the wall for about fifty minutes. He did not know how to work an event. He could have made six new contacts and still had a pint.

Now, you have got six business contacts without much stretch by targeting those you don't know. What next? You need to drop them a note to say "nice to meet you." You may be able to help them by networking them to someone else. This may be the time to send your material. Ask them if they know anyone else who needs your services. The people you met may not need a graphic designer, but if you ask them, they probably know someone who does. You need to ASK for business, – so simple really but not very British. "Courage mon brave"!

◄◄

You need to ASK for business

The all important "follow up" will be covered in chapter five.

Does all this sound an effort? It is, but don't forget the definition of madness, doing the same thing and expecting a different outcome. We are netWORKING and the yields can be outstanding. Be prepared for the effort. How long does it take to write six short cards probably with your logo on it? You could land £60,000 worth of business by finishing the job, so roll-up your sleeves up and don't whinge!

Before we leave the event, one of the most rewarding things you can do is to introduce people, especially women. Most businesswomen are very capable of looking after themselves, and actually tend to be much better networkers than men. However, in a meeting which is predominantly male, a bit of attention to the ladies well-being and enjoyment of the occasion will be much appreciated. They may return to the next event with friends from the business world. They ALWAYS add to the meeting. Conversely, meetings full of men can suffer from the barrack room syndrome, which ALWAYS detracts, and lessens the productiveness of the occasion. I have seen women cringe with embarrassment at such thoughtless and foolish behaviour. They do not return.

◄◄

Enjoy your next event, it could be worth a fortune

Enjoy your next event, it could be worth a fortune.

Measure The Results

One of the most astounding things observed amongst members of BNI is that they sometimes FORGET really valuable referrals. This may be for two reasons. They are turning over £15 million per annum in sales and £150,000 is not a large order and easily lost in the mix, or they become blasé about being referred a stream of opportunity. For a cost of £700 per annum, the £150,000 leaves a reasonable margin.

It is advisable therefore to record your networking activities. It is simple to do on a spread sheet. Record the work referred to you and its value. Normally, people only perceive half the value of work referred to them. One member, a printer, forgot a £23,000 contract within two months, and had to be reminded by someone else.

Keep all the business cards you collect. They may become current in eighteen months time. If you can work them into a computer, with cross- referencing, so much the better. There may be software available.

Keep a record of every referral you receive, and every referral you give. Track them both. Check to see if people referred got the work, in other words, be interested. If it did not work, find out why. Another nudge might make it happen.

By recording, you can make changes and set new and more exciting goals.

Tools Of Networking

At a recent meeting of the Kent International Trade Club, at which I was a guest speaker, I suggested that business cards were very important. One distinguished person, with a strong business, admitted that he had not had one for years. Apparently fired by my short presentation, he vowed to put the matter right.

Over the last five years, it has been amazing to see how many businesses are so poorly represented by their business card, or total lack of.

OK, so business cards are a tool, what else must we have? Essentials are a card holder to display your business card, preferably one which clips to your clothing. Some well organised promotional literature is useful, make it pocket sized so that it does not get bent.

All materials need to be professional in appearance. Despite the possibility of using your PC, it really is better to a get a professional to do it, they come up with some excellent ideas. Make sure, however, that they produce something legible, I see many where colours interfere with the clarity.

◄◄

All materials need to be professional in appearance

A card file is a useful addition, rather than stuffing cards in a jacket pocket, where they may get lost. In Asian countries, the cards should remain visible throughout the conversation. It is rude to hide them away, and a small ceremony takes place as the card is presented by holding with the thumbs of both hands, and a slight bow. Such is the power of business cards!

It is advisable to have cards with your name clearly in the middle. The card should not try to carry much information. However, cyber-type cards are very irritating, not showing an address, only "e" info. People like to know where you come from. You may be too far away to do business, even by e-mail.

Eye catching might be good. It is important to have a recognisable logo, and to be remembered. A clue as to your business is preferable but it needs to be obvious. The card is part of the first impression – thin card, poor graphics, too much information are all raising questions about your professionalism. Spend some money and get it right.

|◀◀

Spend some money and get it right

Chapter Four

CARING ABOUT OTHERS

Give In Order To Receive

Societies the world over have cartwheeled in the last one hundred years. The only constant in life is change. Nothing stays the same. Dynasties come and go.

However the givers in life stand out like lighthouses – Mother Theresa, Gandhi, Nelson Mandela, people of courage and sacrifice. Jesus of Nazareth is the ultimate example.

So it is at a local level. There are always people who do more than their share in all walks of life. They are probably people who sleep easy at night and WON'T be found in politics!

Those of us not so blessed need to take from this example. Men are appallingly bad at listening, which makes referring more difficult. Women care much more at every level.

A. If You Wish To Be Referred You Must First Refer

The payback will almost certainly not be instantaneous. It requires confidence in the person you wish to refer. This may not be immediate either. Try them out, find out about their professionalism, aims, ambitions, interests, other networks etc, and it will be easier. They may well fall down here, good thing you did not refer them at this stage.

B. Learn To Promote Them

Once satisfied they will not tarnish your reputation. If in doubt, don't refer them. You can do a great deal to promote others. There are ten levels of input to a referral. Depending on the

⏮

The payback will almost certainly not be instantaneous

quality of your relationship, you can just refer, or totally pre-sell them. This requires a lot of effort – why go to so much trouble?

The ten levels are:

1 Pass a name – lead.
2 Name and phone number – still a lead/cold call
3 Name, phone number and literature.
4 Testimonial on your behalf. Great but still all to do.
5 Introductory letter. At last, some real effort.
6 Personal phone call. At last a referral.
7 Letter and call – strong referral.
8 Promotion and call – high impact.
9 Arrange meeting – eye to eye.
10 Three way meeting.

C. Understanding Relationships In Business

Nowadays "relationship" is an overworked word. This is ironic, because at social and business level, it is not well understood.

There has been a marked improvement since the 1980's, when need and greed inspired business people to behave in an unsustainable and totally selfish way.

Relationships need to be examined. Many business people are totally unaware of the law of "cause and effect." They suffer from effects which they don't like, because their behaviour with another has precipitated that effect, ie they caused it!

Relationships tend to be fragile and easily undermined. Unguarded comments, rudeness, excessive demands, late payment without just cause, late start dates, failure to communicate or to return calls, all cause erosion. Examples are endless.

Good relationships with other businesses are actually easy to maintain and even strengthen. The old adage "people buy from people" is an accurate account of cultivated relationships, in other words, the chemistry is right.

◄◄

People buy from people on account of cultivated relationships

Within the BNI organisation, a "strong contact" culture with a high frequency of contact, relationship building becomes an art form. Business owners meet, and are trained to do so, with a view to discussing each other's business, and ways to develop a symbiotic relationship.

The more they meet, the deeper the bond and the easier it becomes to refer each other to the all important third party.

The problem is always going to be that the majority you deal with don't have the skills you might just be acquiring yourself. This leads to a need to educate others not necessarily in self-development mode. Lead by example and be patient. When stressed with too much work, how about passing some useful business to your major competitor? Done the right way, the competitor will be grateful. How will they view you now? Especially if you say "you are the only company I can trust to make a good job of this!" A relationship just moved from low/non-existent to one of potential co-operation, or dialogue at least.

D. Professionalism In SMEs

How does your company appear to others and does it matter anyway? In a competitive world it is shocking to see companies so unaware of the impact, positive or negative, they have on the world at large. Most business owners arrived through "the school of hard knocks" and not from Harvard, the LSE or Sorbonne. They have never received education about presentation skills, marketing, or any business skills at all. Some become educated via the internet, to the extent that advice from that quarter is useful, or has its own agenda.

Company standards, such as the ISO 9000 scheme, have given tremendous impetus to the acquisition of a professional basis, which will be key in developing the confidence of others as they begin a relationship with your company. "Confidence and relationship" are inextricably linked.

E. Other Methods To Become More Professional – Show You Care About Yourself
1. Materials

Materials used need to be of a high order. Saving money on promotional assets is not a good plan – graphic designers will take an idea and win you new business. Poor materials will make you look cheap.

Before you spend money, develop a sound strategy – maybe you need to take advice from a marketing expert? Before you take advice, ask around to get an expert, with testimonials from people you know. This all needs budgeting but a good strategy can pay handsomely. Jay Abraham, the self-taught American marketing guru charges hugely, but his effectiveness and perception make him worthwhile. He charges £9,000 per hour on the phone! He was once asked to assist with a TV advertisement which was about 60% effective. In a seven word slogan, he juxtaposed two words with a 300% return on expectation. Worth his money?

2. Techniques

There are ways to do more professional presentations. I sit through forty minutes of presentations per week, and have done for five years. This makes me a well qualified observer. I see the effective range from exceptional, enlightened, to the crass end. In nearly all cases, it boils down to preparation, and the degrees to which business people value this opportunity.

⏮

In nearly all cases,
it boils down to
preparation

Remember every time you speak to an audience, you actually have an audience with three different listening mechanisms. You will fall into one yourself, your dialogue will represent whether you are:

AUDITORY – relying on words to convey or receive messages.

VISUAL – using pictures, images, visual words "do you <u>see</u> what I mean?"

KINESTHETIC – touchy feely, relying on deep feeling, "I know how you <u>feel</u>".

The audience will be in three parts. Learn to use all three communication types and you will be received by 90% of the audience.

To present in a professional way, business people must be prepared to continue to educate themselves. Much has been written about this subject, any quality bookshop will carry useful material. Simply being aware will help. Here are some ideas.

Power Point Presentations

About one in five people can do a power presentation. Most over run, or under run the script. To be good – practice, practice, then practice some more.

Interactive White Board

These are a recent creature of technology, and although only exposed to it on a few occasions, this is an impressive addition.

Laptop Controlled Slide Show

This is a most professional way to convey a message, now in common usage. Beware laptops don't always deliver, they get stage fright in front of an audience. What is your **back up** presentation like? You need an alternative method with you – flip chart, whiteboard etc. You look like an idiot if the laptop fails, and you are unable to get at your own material – an opportunity wasted. **Don't rely on technology** – be professional, be prepared.

Personal Professionalism

Some Tips To Demonstrate Care

a. Avoid bad language – it is very disempowering

b. Dress appropriately. You are judged by your outward appearance. It is not PC, but ultimately we are cautious animals. Until a relationship exists we are judged 80% by our body language. Dress is an outward manifestation of your inner workings. Shabby kills relationships! Shoes reflect your station in life, or at least your value of it. Make sure you make the most of yourself. Tie at half-mast? School children look tatty with shirts untucked.

c. Personal hygiene. It is simply inexcusable to be

◀◀

Make sure you make the most of yourself

unkempt these days. I recently heard of a lucrative contract being lost because a company's employee turned up to a job with appalling body odour. Tatty hair, clothes with mended holes, dirty clothes all show a lack of CARE.

d   Sexist jokes – laddish behaviour. I have been running a crusade within the BNI organisation to stamp out sexist jokes, sexually based jokes, innuendo, and excessive laddish behaviour. Within a group, this behaviour does a tremendous amount of harm. It demonstrates total lack of care for the female members, who literally cringe when this sort of thing breaks out. They don't say so, they don't do anything about it, they simply don't continue any sort of relationship with the filth monger. Men, save all that stuff for the rugby club, if you must wallow in it. Preferably, just grow up!

e. Say "thank you". Recognise and reward referees. You don't know how lucky you are when someone has taken you "on board" – they are out there helping you to advance your business. How powerful is that?

i.   The first thing you do is to keep them updated about how it went.

ii. Tell them what you are doing next.

iii. Constant updates. This REALLY builds relationships and demonstrates CARE. Maybe send them a small present? A complimentary offering? Pass information about your family and ask them about theirs. By doing these things, you will quickly strengthen the relationship – all by CARING!

iv. Rewards. When you have turned a referral into a customer, you must at least recognise this fact to the source. You may wish to reward them. Here are some tips with regard to rewards.

■ Members of BNI will want to return the favour with a productive referral.

■ Develop ways to reward the source. It may be a dinner for two, theatre tickets, public acclaim at an appropriate moment. It may even be a cash incentive, or discounts on your services. I always have an issue that prices charged should be identical for referred business and the source. Different pricing can lead to disappointment. If the price was the strong point and different prices are charged, value will be dissimilar.

■ Work out when to provide the reward.

■ When will this be presented? At referral, or closed deal?

- Go for something they don't do for themselves. For instance everybody in the UK travels these days – not a great gift anymore.
- Try to remember what you have done. You may need to do something different next time.
- Whatever you do – do something each time, or you will turn off the source.

Rewarding will definitely speed up what can be a lengthy process.

Rewarding will definitely speed up what can be a lengthy process

Dealing With Challenges

It's a fact of life – things do go wrong. The caring business owner recognises that by dealing with things that have not gone to hand gives them the opportunity to demonstrate their caring attitude. Handled well, this can actually be turned into an advantageous situation. With poor attitude, litigation can follow.

■ Inappropriate referral

Sometimes, a referral may be inappropriate. How do you deal with it? You may have wasted time and money.

You need to examine what has happened? If it is the first referral from a new source, they have just started working for you. That is a great moment. Proceed with caution! Great tact is required. The best thing you can do is to take the new referrer to lunch. At the lunch, firstly ask how you can help them. Secondly, with enormous diplomacy, tell them you are grateful for their first effort, and point out exactly what it is you want. It is probably your fault they got it wrong – they did not know exactly what you wanted.

■ Execution of a referral which went wrong

Every business has its challenges. Occasionally, the job goes wrong. The caring business owner immediately takes responsibility and puts a plan of retrieval into action. Backed with excellent communication, and a good attitude of "how can we put this right?", the compromised party will be encouraged to deal with you again. They may even refer you to others.

■ Finance-related problems

I am constantly amazed at how many companies give extended credit to customers without agreements. Keeping funds in the business is important. There are factoring arrangements, and businesses specialising in debt recovery, both extremely effective. Get organised, it is YOUR money. Over-pricing, late payments, contract failure and disputes are a fact of life. In the referred environment such things occur much less frequently. This is due to the existence of a relationship, and therefore knowledge. Nobody is going to refer anyone to a failing business – at least not knowingly.

Should this happen, normal channels for recovery will be required. In five years with BNI, I have only come across a couple of such disputes a year, and with a network spanning 2,000 companies, that must be statistically very small.

Learning To Listen.
Take An Interest In Others

CRUNCH TIME. So you think you care about others? Huh? WRONG! The most important sound in the entire world is our own name. Men, women, children and goldfish for all I know – crave to hear their name!

Women are reasonably good listeners – men are hopeless! This is not a sexist observation but well documented. Books have been written about it.

When you see a group photograph – whose face do you look for first? Yours of course!

If we merely try to impress people and get people interested in us, we are going to end up friendless. Napoleon was one such. He is quoted in his last meeting with the famous Boulonnaise, Josephine, "Josephine, I have been as fortunate as any man ever was on earth and yet, at this hour, you are the only person on whom I can rely." And he was wrong about that too, as she cheated on him.

Alfred Adler, the Viennese psychologist, wrote a book "What Life Should Mean to You." In it he says "It is the individual who is not interested in his fellow men who has the greatest difficulties in life and provides the greatest injury to others. It is from among such individuals that all human failures spring." Many despots and tyrants fit the mould – the list would be long and depressing.

We can train ourselves to be interested. The self-development expert Brian Tracey produced a fascinating technique. If you are being subjected to a piece that is difficult to get interested in, you must pretend it is the most interesting thing you ever heard. After two or three minutes, the tedium lifts; after five minutes, you may actually become interested if you have concentrated on the pretence. In other words, YOU CAN TRAIN YOUR MIND.

I had to train my mind to LISTEN. I was a poor listener, but after five years of interaction with quality business professionals, I now pride myself on my listening abilities. The pay-back is enormous. I had to acquire the skill.

By listening, you will become genuinely interested in others. When we are in trouble, we need a sympathetic listener. That is all an irritated customer, a dissatisfied employee or a hurt friend wants.

⏮

By listening, you will become genuinely interested in others

The largest value business passed between members of one group of business people happened at Tonbridge in Kent, England. A seemingly unimportant member – a small scale family printer, was a good listener. He overheard his sister talking to a friend – which resulted in him asking questions. He referred £4.5 million to a grateful fellow member. A few weeks previously, a visitor cited this small scale business as a reason not to join. He felt the printers business insignificant, and not capable of passing anything worthwhile to anyone else! He also failed to see the NETWORK of contacts as a resource.

I remember, as a young man, being crushed by adverse comments from someone I greatly admired. The comment came back to me from a third party that I was a frightful bore! In my youthful enthusiasm, I had talked <u>at</u> this person, exposing my huge ego, not once asking a question or showing any interest in this hero figure.

Self-evident I guess. You don't need qualification to see that asking questions and listening intently to the answers is very caring, and rewarding.

Remembering People's Names

As a farmer, I had a pitifully small contact sphere. Long hours, a shrinking industry, fatigue, social isolation all led to a small life. It was easy to remember the few people I came across, and those I did not remember, too bad, I did not care.

Once re-launched into the world of commerce and PEOPLE, this failure to remember names became a real issue. I once heard a speaker give some indications as to how to improve. It sounded a bit 'over the top', but once mastered, yielded colossal results. I now have a good grasp of nearly 2,000 names but it becomes more difficult in Malaysia, where the names are not written as they sound to the Western ear.

Here are some simple tips to improve your ability to remember names.

1. Repeat the new name in full several times in the conversation.
2. Find a syllable in the name which has some connotation to the occupation. For instance Simon Evenden the Dentist – a bit obvious but it works.
3. If you have the business card, look at it as you watch and listen to that person give a presentation – works very well for me.
4. Physical appearance.

You will build relationships very quickly if you can master this. On the other hand, you will damage relationships if you get people's names wrong. Better to admit you have forgotten than try to duck the issue, you look really stupid if you do that!

"What was the reason for Andrew Carnegie's success? He was called the Steel King; yet he himself knew little about the manufacture of steel. He had hundreds of people working for him who knew far more about steel than he did.

But he knew how to handle people, and that is what made him rich. Early in life, he showed a flair for organization, a genius for leadership. By the time he was ten, he too had discovered the astounding importance people place on their own name. And he used that discovery to win cooperation.

To illustrate: When he was a boy back in Scotland, he got hold of a rabbit, a mother rabbit. Presto! He soon had a whole nest of little rabbits – and nothing to feed them. But he had a brilliant idea. He told the boys and girls in the neighbourhood that if they would go out and pull enough clover and dandelions to feed the rabbits, he would name the bunnies in their honour."

|◀◀

Never forget names, it is an easy way to demonstrate you care

Chapter Five

CHOICE OF LANGUAGE – DO ACTIONS SPEAK LOUDER THAN WORDS?

Do you know what percentage of a spoken communication is conveyed by the words used? It is a staggeringly small 7%. The rest of the message is conveyed by body language ie the animal part, the conscious communication. What do I mean?

■ Tonality. Includes emphasis, speed of delivery, if the voice moves up and down, or stays dead pan. This will demonstrate truth or deceit.

- Eye contact. Was this strong, weak, non-existent, flat, animated? Did the eyes match voice and body?
- Facial expressions. Fearful, aggressive, evasive, happy, mad, sad – so many!
- Body posture. Was the body erect and energetic or slumped and beaten, indifferent, moving or still?

This chapter is going to deal with choice of language.

⏮

Every single one of us has a distinct pattern of words we use

Becoming Aware

How many of us are aware that we all construct our words differently? Every single one of us has a distinct pattern of words we use. Some of us are very successful, some of us are extremely unsuccessful. Do those two types use the same words? Most definitely, they do not! Do our circumstances such as education, family background, general experience have an effect? Yes, most definitely. Can we change? Yes, most definitely. Every word uttered needs to be recalled by the brain, so we can all change the way we construct our communications.

First of all we need to listen to ourselves. Most speech is more or less automatic, but we all have two voices, the external and the most used of the two – 'the internal chatter box'. This is the little voice which talks to us all the time and which has as much effect on us as the external voice has on other people.

Let me give an example of the internal voice. It is the voice which persuades a cigarette smoker hell bent on giving up smoking, to have "just one more, it won't hurt!" It is the voice which encourages someone wanting to shed some pounds, to buy a nice confectionery bar, or have some chocolate. It is also the voice which carries a sportsman to victory against the odds, if the sportsman has learnt how to use the voice to his advantage.

In other words, it chatters on, one way or the other, for good or for bad, regardless. It can be trained to work for the good, it can restore people to health, it can defeat cancer, it can transform someone from poverty to financial independence.

Either way, it just chatters on constantly.

Why Should We Bother? People Know What We Mean

The words we choose to use are a direct window into the soul. The fact that we DON'T control our words means that others know exactly what we think about ourselves.

Does that matter? What if the chattering voice repeatedly tells us we are a failure? We will use the words of failure. It may be a parent, partner or sibling is constantly telling us we are a failure, and we may start to believe this. We then start to use failure type words and phrases "I can't...", "I don't...", "I won't...", "I couldn't" – all peppered with negativity.

Sadly, these influences might have been heaped on us from birth, or at an early stage.

⏮

The words we use have an enormous impact on others

The words we use have an enormous impact on others. I am allergic to negative people, I run a mile from people whose language is DIS-EMPOWERING. Their negativity destroys my high energy levels.

It was not always like that. When my farming career was failing, I became negative and used

DIS-EMPOWERING language. It was a time when people did not relate well to me. I was acutely aware of this antipathy, but that only made me more negative.

Fortunately for me, I stumbled across the "self-development" industry, and read books like "How to Win Friends and Influence People" by D. Carnegie, "Think and Grow Rich", by Napoleon Hill, and "Unleash the Power Within" Anthony Robbins. I was sufficiently fascinated to read and ACT.

If you want people to take you seriously, to win a sales order, find a spouse, have a great social life, preach a religion, be a politician, first MASTER YOUR LANGUAGE.

Empowering Language

What is the difference between a problem and a challenge? There isn't any! But packaged as a problem, it might seem impossible, difficult, hard, worrying, frightening. If we refer to the 'problem', as a 'situation' or a 'challenge', we are immediately looking for a way round, rather than suffering from inertia. Challenges are usually fun, problems are unsolvable and forbidding. The difference is simply the words you choose to use.

Another word which disempowers so many is 'boring'. Financial people are somehow ashamed of the nature of their business. But we ALL need their services.

A way to empower this is to look at some alternatives.

Unhelpful adjectives	Some positive alternatives
Boring	Exacting – we all want to know an exacting financier
Small	Personal/Growing
Problems	Challenges
Disaster	Situation
Small	Dedicated

Virgin Atlantic started small, as a 'two man band'. Small? – Well-founded!

When preparing a presentation, ask yourself how the audience would judge your words, as you yourself are aware of other people's language.

Is you language empowering and attractive, or negative and repellant?

Positive Or Negative?

Most companies experience continued challenges. Do you colour your experiences positive or negative? The words you use will tell others how you feel about your business. When asked how business is, how about saying "Great!"

Such positive stuff is encouraging. If you say "could be better", some will construe you are going bust, and may place the business elsewhere.

In order to become aware of how you express yourself, let me give you an exercise. For the next thirty days – make a point of listening to others, and note their choice of words. Do the words help them, or hinder them? A new habit takes thirty days to acquire. At the end of this time, you will be aware of the impact your choice of words has on others.

Is you language empowering and attractive, or negative and repellant?

Chapter Six

NON VERBAL COMMUNICATION

Why is it some politicians are a terrible flop on TV? Some are brilliant. Either way, it is a tragedy for the voting public. Some excellent public servants never get to serve because of this. Some vacuous actors with no political talent get to rule, because they come across strongly in front of camera, uttering someone else's words and borrowing ideas from where ever.

It is all down to their skill at managing their 'state'. We all have a state of 'being' – you have one right now as you read. The majority of us are born without a gift for public speaking, it comes with practice. More confident people give themselves more opportunity – the joker in the school classroom, the wag with a funny quip during a Wimbledon tennis match.

My own experience was one of excruciating shyness as a child. I often had the right answer for the teacher but would NEVER offer it unless asked directly. I now speak strongly in public on a daily basis. How can you reconcile this extreme? My passage was through form captain to house captain and prefect at school, on to college to be aghast at standing as President of the Students' Union, and being voted in! What a growth curve.

I then served on community bodies, and became Vice-Chairman of a large Trade Organisation, and from there to Executive Director of BNI, with responsibility for training in front of hundreds of people. I am nervous every time I speak – but I have come to realise there is always a result, good or bad, and that usually the audience WANTS YOU TO DO WELL! So let's examine what secrets we give away with our bodies when we speak.

◄◄

So let's examine what secrets we give away with our bodies when we speak

1. Tonality

Mostly, our speech rises and falls. Some people are masters at emphasising points with tonality. If you add to this changes in speed of delivery, you end up with great orators like Churchill who galvanised British resolve; Gandhi, who influenced 200 million people; Nelson Mandela, who gained worldwide support for his campaign. Sadly, tyrants are good at this too. Hitler, Napoleon, the madman Mussolini, and some still on today's world stage.

2. Eye Contact

I once had to address 4,000 at a convention. What a terrifying ordeal for an excruciatingly shy person. What happens to you? The heart rate soars, the mouth goes bone dry BEFORE you even get on stage, and the legs just become detached. They work, but not in unison.

As you take the stage, you can't see anyone but you are aware, in the dimness, of a sea of 'cabbages', all stacked neatly in rows – the pale faces of audience. Your brain totally disconnects from the well rehearsed and prepared piece. Abject panic is a nano-second below the surface. With immense resolve, the eye is dragged back to the script, and your voice starts. It sounds like a bull roaring. As you grow accustomed to the light, you see the faces are actually smiling. You feel a weeny bit better. You make a reasonable start, and the mouth is still dry, with ALL feeling having deserted your legs, the knees knock. BUT . . . you try a small joke, and you hear the audience laugh. You suddenly feel OK! You try another joke, and suddenly you see the audience are having a good time and you become unstoppable. Because of great preparation, you finish on the minute, and receive tremendous applause. It is a full twenty minutes before the hands stop shaking and the heart rate drops to normal.

What happens that enables you to pull it off? Eye contact. In fact you only connected with several of the 4,000 by eye. With the smiling faces, the eyes connect. It really is the human contact. Having done a couple of TV interviews, it is definitely not as easy in front of the dead pan camera.

When addressing a meeting, make eye contact with as many listeners as possible. Move around if you can so that you make eye contact with those in the poorer

◄◄

When addressing a meeting, make eye contact with as many listeners as possible

seats. It is very difficult for an audience to doze off if the speaker is making eye contact with them. They then get much more out of the presentation.

Some do's and don't's

1. Do spread the eye contact around the room.
2. Do look up from time to time while reading a script. This requires knowing the script well so you don't lose your place and get flustered.
3. Do have a 'smile in the eyes' – it is very "seductive" to an audience.
4. Avoid looking at your shoe laces – admits the fear and shows a feeling of inferiority.
5. Failure to make any eye contact is shifty and might suggest you don't believe in your script.
6. Avoid looking a the ceiling – suggests haughtiness.
7. Avoid too much eye contact with one or two people, especially if he/she is visually blessed. Others will note this.
8. Avoid burying your head in the script – that just looks inept.
9. Avoid looking out of the window – the audience will assume that is where you would rather be.

3. Facial Expression

Much is conveyed by the face. The National Director for BNI in Canada, Don Morgan, gave a tremendous address some years ago on "Facial Aerobics" – highly amusing, but essential to Directors of the BNI organisation. BNI tradition is to meet early in the morning, and Don is aware that we can sit in our cars with a pasty, tired, washed-out appearance as we meet with our members. Don's antidote is to limber up the face with aerobic excercises.

A. The most critical facial expression is the <u>SMILE</u>. My goodness, how much is a smile worth? A nicely limbered-up face at 6:30am can produce a lovely smile. What do you get if you smile? 99% of the time you get one back... and now YOU are feeling good too! Our day is beginning to really TAKE OFF. Why is it, in this abundant society of the Western World, so many look so miserable? What happened to the SMILE?

⏮

What do you get if you smile? 99% of the time you get one back

As BNI Directors of Operations in Malaysia, the authors have noted endlessly, that an emerging nation, with much less opportunity, although developing fast, has one of the happiest countenances in the world. The Malaysian smile will captivate you, it comes so readily, and is so genuine. I urge the reader to visit that beautiful country.

B. To register displeasure. The police are good at this. The dead pan traffic policeman makes you feel an abject criminal as you get booked for speeding. How about the beaten look on the faces of sports fans as their team gets a thrashing? OR sheer happiness on the face of an Olympic athlete winning the Gold medal; it goes way beyond a smile. How about disgust, demonstrated by those being put out of work – FURY and fear mixed together.

C. To register surprise – facial muscles pull upwards.

D. To register fear – muscles tighten and eyes widen.

E. To register sexual interest – pupils widen, probably to admit more of this pleasing countenance to the brain!

Clearly there are many complex facial expressions. Experts made one outstanding discovery.

The face takes on a particular look. Then the person then takes on that feeling.

The significance is that if you feel bad, but make yourself smile, then you will immediately feel better. Learn to control facial expression – first become aware by watching others. This accounts for 35% of non-verbal communication.

4. Body Posture

Whatever our own bearing, others are aware of it, and how they feel about us

We all have a distinct carriage. All humans are basically the same – two legs, a backbone, and a head on the top. But we all have a different bearing. Some walk very erect with a military appearance, others are round shouldered and slumped, some walk with speed and purpose and others shuffle along. Whatever our own bearing and gait, others are aware of it, and particularly how they feel about us. We are essentially animals, and we make sub-conscious notes about those around us. It is not the definitive judgement, but an important part of it.

We can all see posture in two teams locked in competition. In rugby terms, the losing side are often described as having "their heads down." This is an admission of defeat, even before the game is over.

As I write in 2002, the English cricket team has in recent times been beaten by all comers. The "Body Language" of the players communicated defeat, even before the game began. Their self-belief was so low it reflected in their posture. American tennis players reflect the opposite. They always appear to carry their bodies in such a way as to suggest "defeat is impossible." Their self-belief is so strong it shows in their posture. The opponent is all too aware of it, and this may reflect in their own body language. Occasionally one player in a team will display different body language to the rest of the team, as they don't fall in with their team mates level of belief. Two such English players are the cricketer Ian Botham, whose belief won matches, and David Beckham, the footballer, who continually lifts the morale of his team, with great belief – communicated to his team mates and the opposition by – you guessed it, body language.

We need to be aware of body posture

We need to be aware of body posture. When you are uncomfortable – does your body resemble a knot done by a boy scout? Do you sometimes look too laid back? Communicating you can't be bothered, or this is unimportant to me. Perhaps, we need to appear laid back rather that knotted or anxious. If you were being interviewed by the Inland Revenue – much tension appearing in your body language would almost certainly arouse suspicion that you had something to hide.

I met an interesting New York Attorney a few years ago. His name is Richard Green, and he has become an expert on body language. I attended a seminar of his in November in the UK. The following March, I attended a seminar in Dallas, at which O.J. Simpson, the famous American athelete, talked about success mentality. A few weeks later he was indicted and charged with murdering his wife.

At his trial, the full blast of democracy was employed with the case being televised. Every evening, a panel of experts would pore over the day's proceedings. One of the experts was Richard Green. His brief was to examine O.J. Simpson in the witness box. He could tell if the defendant was lying by checking O.J. Simpson's body language.

In other words, were the answers given by Simpson congruent with the way his body moved and postured?

5. Dress As A Means Of Communication

We live in much more enlightened and egalitarian times. The formal wear of Victorian times has given way to a much more casual approach.

Does it really matter what we wear any more? It is not very straightforward nowadays but the best answer is yes, at times, it still matters.

|◀◀
Whatever we choose to wear, it is a statement

Whatever we choose to wear, it is a statement. Teenagers are driven by peer pressure to follow fashion. Recent trends are for young men to wear woolly hats over the ears, even in hot weather. They usually carry a skate board – the whole package denotes "cool-dude"! If a sixty year old woman behaved and dressed like that, people would be taken to hospital with laughter attacks!

If anybody was referred to a medical surgeon, who was to be found in short trousers and a singlet vest with heavily tattooed arms, with open-toed sandals, they would almost certainly have no confidence that this person was a capable medical expert.

If you wanted to refer a computer expert to a Chief Executive of a PLC, you would need to feel confident that the expert would attend the meeting looking like a serious professional. If the expert attended the meeting in a tee shirt with a dead beat slogan, and dirty jeans, it would be the last referral they ever got from you!

The old adage "dress up to go up" was never more appropriate than now. I once attended an awards ceremony which was black tie. Sadly, I forgot mine as I packed the car. I turned up in a black tee shirt, and white trousers. I might have got away with it, except I won THE major award. My dress could have been interpreted badly, ie I don't care about this event, or these people, and let's get to the party as soon as this is wrapped up! As it happens the opposite was true, and part of my acceptance speech had to be an apology.

Had I been the only one in black tie, it would not have been embarrassing.

My advice is to check out your wardrobe. However politically correct you are, others take mental notes about YOUR appearance, and may make harsh silent judgements.

Shoes have been highlighted as an insight into character. How many would be happy taking advice from a financier whose shoes were badly worn, or very cheap?

How many people would be happy to see a doctor whose shoes were filthy dirty? Dirty fingernails? Greasy, unkempt hair?

What about personal hygiene? I recently heard that a wealthy woman turned away a tradesman from a lucrative job, because his mate had appalling body odour? It may have been an unfortunate medical condition, or just slovenliness. Who wants to investigate? Nobody!

|◀◀

Do you care about your appearance? You had better if you want to get on

Do you care about your appearance? You had better if you want to get on.

Chapter Seven

NURTURE THE RELATIONSHIP

Reward The Referrer

(see also part one chapter four)

"I would rather have 1% of 100 people's effort than 100% of my own." John Paul Getty.

Here is a man who understood the dynamics of human nature.

We spend a great deal of effort getting others to help us out, only to damage the chance of on-going support by small acts of thoughtlessness or omission.

During five years of intense business networking, I have been amazed at how easily people give up tremendous gains they have made. A member from a networking group in Sussex, England gained £100,000 of business per annum. The group lost a few members through attrition. Some effort was required to replace them. Instead of going "ballistic" to repair the group, this member left too! Where do you go and what do you do to replace the £100,000? An Advert in the Parish magazine?

A conversation with a member who received about £60,000 of referred business gave new insight into complacency. This member was naturally very excited about networking at the outset, with a great deal of enthusiasm for the substantial return on time invested. He met other members on a one to one basis, he attended trainings and social events. He referred business to others.

However, three years down the line, he intimated it wasn't yielding as it used to. Following some probing and gentle enquiry, he had stopped some of the activities. Firstly, he no longer "rewarded" the referrer. He passed them business and thanked them. He did not "buy dinner for two", give theatre tickets, treat them to lunch. He stopped meeting one to one, particularly the new member businesses in his group, and he admitted to only attending "socials" occasionally.

He effectively diluted his own input. What happens if you "effectively dilute the effort at the office?" ie work two days a week. Your income goes down, that's what!

At a BNI meeting, I once saw an attractive woman walk round a table in a room full of people, to give a referral to a young man. Clearly, she was pleased that she had a worthwhile referral to give to the landscape gardener. He continued looking in front as she passed behind, and held his hand up to receive the details on paper. He did not look at her, he did not say "thank you", he read the details and continued to study what was in front of himself.

He sent a message to thirty two local business people. What was that message? "I wish I was somewhere else. I don't care about you lot!" The

◄◄

What happens if you "effectively dilute the effort at the office?" Your income goes down

massive power of the unspoken message. Ouch! No more referrals for you, my lad!

Many times I have seen members who understand that these relationships need constant attention, gain phenomenal rewards. A valued member in one such group had scant return for a whole year, but developed a caring attitude for those around him. After three years, he received a referral for £956,000, a years work for his company.

Mark Keatley-Palmer, partner of a Graphic Design Consultancy and founder member of his BNI chapter, served his group well, and took several turns chairing the meeting. He regularly introduced new business to the group, and one day received a referral for on-going work worth many £100,000's. Now a five year member of BNI, his dedication to networking and his chapter continues unabated.

Networking is <u>not</u> a social activity. It involves socialising and is fun. It is not social as an end in itself. It is hugely enjoyable, much more so than work. It is work. For many, it is marketing activity for their company, especially for the small company.

What is a reasonable reward for a referral that generated business? That will depend on many things, lets try to list them.

1. How much business was involved?
2. How much effort went into getting it?
3. How many referrals have come from the source?
4. The scale of your operation.
5. The depth of your pocket.
6. The quality of the relationship.
7. Previous rewards to the source.

I am sure there are more. However, you need to be sensitive. If you are perceived as wealthy, and give too insignificant a reward, that in itself may be worse than no reward at all.

At the very least, one needs to say a sincere "thank you", OR erosion may set in whatever you do. Give it plenty of thought.

Avoid Erosion

We have just instanced situations which can erode or DAMAGE relationships. I see this too often, so let's become aware of how to avoid losing what you have worked hard to establish.

1. Be Consistent

Blowing hot and cold is a certain way to lose credibility. If you do this in your business generally you will fail, so don't mess with your network.

BNI expects members to represent their company fifty one times per annum. We feel that a missed meeting leads to six weeks diminished return, that is, the group has cooled towards the absentee, FOR SIX WEEKS. Don't do it!

⏮

With more casual networks, don't miss meetings

With more casual networks, don't miss meetings, or be late. It is <u>very</u> aggravating.

2. Be Prepared

Lack of preparation shows. If you appear unprepared, will you go to meet the new contact less than perfectly prepared. Almost certainly!

You need to be very organised and allocate the time necessary to achieve that state. If you are expected to present at a meeting, prepare your speech, and any collateral material. It should be well-presented. Poor materials are a strong source of EROSION. Be aware of how others see you!

3. Watch Your Tongue

The poorly chosen word can minimise your chances of being referred, even when spoken in jest. One excellent member ended his membership with a dreadful remark "thanks for the referral, I was able to stitch that customer up like a christmas turkey!" Ha ha, hilarious. There was a deathly hush and his referral source, thirty of them, dried up totally from that moment.

Avoid shouting out during meetings. Every group has its comedian, sometimes loved, sometimes feared, sometimes hated, nearly always lowering the value of the occasion. Business people are not looking for entertainment – their time is too precious. However, natural good humour is attractive. As with all things in life, balance is the key. THINK WITH YOUR BRAIN, NOT YOUR MOUTH!

4. Keep Up The Communication

If you want the referrals to keep coming, you need to be high profile – that is, continue to communicate, email, phone, Christmas cards etc. Don't let them forget you!

Which leads us on to . . .

Learn About Them In Great Depth

If you wish to refer others (and if you wish to be referred, presumably you do) you need to know lots about them. You will only refer others when you are confident in their ability to deliver, and you are confident in their passion about what they do.

Sorry about this... there are NO short cuts. You simply need to meet them at their work place AND over lunch. How on earth do we find time for all this? Simple. Prioritise. We know they hold the key (probably) to some great new business, so be prepared to invest some time.

◄◄

Confidence means security of knowledge

Referring becomes second nature once you have confidence. Confidence means security of knowledge, which means referrals. Do the ground work.

Refer Them Quality Opportunities

Once you have taken the trouble to find out about people you may want to refer, you will have lots of knowledge about what THEY want. It may not smack you in the face, or even turn up at all. You may have to go find it for them. Sometimes this requires a few phone calls. Sometimes it requires months of effort. Once you have spent months helping someone else, you will see how rewarding it is, and this will inspire you to repeat the exercise. Just assume every referral to someone else will require a good deal of effort.

If you want to receive a good quality referral, you must expect to give a good one. If you find some light weight business, communicate this message to them. ALWAYS evaluate the quality of whatever you pass. The more you communicate the better the chance that you will find exactly the right thing.

Remember, pass heavy-weight referrals, and that is what you will get in return.

Now you are really Networking!

How To Achieve The Ultimate Pre-Sold Job

Setting out, you may not be comfortable referring others. But confidence increases with time. Don't beat yourself up, and master the following:

1. Pass a name. This is a lead, and can be valuable. It takes no effort, and is comfort zone!
2. Name and phone number. Not very adventurous!
3. Name, phone number and promotional literature. This demonstrates a bit of effort involved. Well done, we have made a start.
4. As above, but with a personal testimonial. This has now become a referral. However, there is still much more we can do.
5. As above, but the process starts this time with an introductory letter. Some real effort has now been put into getting a great referral for your contact.
6. Personal phone call. Our contacts phone call to the third party will be expected with anticipation. This is a full on referral - we have arrived!
7. Phone call follows the letter. This is a strong referral, and has a 60% chance of getting business.
8. Send promotional material plus letter. Follow with a call. This is high impact, and at last we are pre-selling. Yes!
9. Arrange a meeting between the referred and the third party. They will both be impressed with the energy you have invested in them both.
10. Three way meeting. You get them together, and

have lunch with them! Good fun, you are totally committed to making business happen. You are a great GIVER... congratulations! A variation on this theme is to take your contact with you to meet your clients. This could be a days outing together.

Take Them Out For The Day To Meet Your Clients

"The power of two". The best decision I ever made was to offer Andrew Hall a partnership. I had been in a partnership before, and had seen at first hand the difficulties and pitfalls – and lived. Together, Andrew and I have probably achieved four times the amount either of us could have done alone. I now have a deep respect and invaluable friendship.

Similarly, if you team up for the day with a "partner" – someone who has referred you strong business, and take them to meet your strongest clients and customers, you will be amazed at the "electricity" it generates. You are demonstrating great "form" to both parties, particularly if your "buddy for the day" has a service or business that is pertinent to the client / customer. The buddy will have face to face introductions, with testimonials etc, and the client sees you promoting a highly recommended source. He / she may be hoping you will do the same for him / her one day!

This is a day sure to bring many rewards.

Keep In Touch

This is so obvious, but guess what? Here lies the greatest erosion of that lovely relationship. Many things cause this serious omission – apparent lack of interesting news, a de-focusing event (marriage, birth etc, launch of new enterprise, illness), inefficiency, systems failure, lack of system etc.

Never ASSUME. That stands for "make an ASS out of U and ME!" What sounds un-newsworthy to you, may be interesting to others.

Christmas cards are a great way to keep in touch with useful people. Many companies produce a newsletter – my accountant sends out a newsletter with interesting information, updates, helpful tips. At some stage, that will win new business, but more

◄◄

Many companies produce a newsletter

importantly help to retain existing business – simply by keeping in touch. Andrew Hall's example of a highly professional salesman of a Boeing 747 is the classic example of keeping in touch. (see page 178)

An excellent way to keep in touch is to set up a time to call your best sources, say once a month. This could be on the pretext "can you update ME about your business – is there anything in particular I could help you with? " A word of warning – be genuine! If you are not, it will be obvious and the relationship will be OVER.

Large organisations take this to extremes in the guise of "customer relations". They do serious hospitality at sporting and entertainment events. It is a way of keeping in touch. Think about this the next time you attend any event – would my great referrer like to enjoy this occasion too? Football, rugby, pop extravaganza could all be great ways to "keep in touch".

BNI meetings are held weekly – BNI knows the value of keeping in touch.

Chapter Eight

GOAL SETTING. PREPARE TO GROW YOUR BUSINESS

Everything I have ever achieved has been by goal setting. This subject warrants a book of its own.

I am indebted to two people in particularly for teaching me how to set goals. The first is Brian Tracey, with a tape I bought by chance on a late night motorway drive to keep me awake! It made me sit bolt upright. It had not finished when I got home. I sat in the drive until it finished at 1:30am.

This tape is also a book, entitled "The Psychology of Achievement" – a must for anyone who has great plans, and also for those, like me, who had not "rung the bell" at that stage.

The second is Zig Ziglar – a curious name for a Texan. I actually heard Zig on stage in Dallas – exceptional material, delivered in a famous Texan drawl.

I learnt from both these sources that goals MUST be written down with a date by which they should be achieved. They must be in the present tense, ie "I have...", "I do...", "I am..." – never "I will...", "I would like to...".

They must never include a negative. "I don't...", "I won't...". You have to understand this positive written message works on the lower brain, the subconscious.

Unfortunately, the subconscious works continuously on the predominant thoughts in your conscious, or upper brain. It does not screen out negative thoughts which might be harmful, it simply works on what you concentrated on.

By <u>writing</u> and dating your goals – the subconscious goes to work and delivers. The goals should be written out in the morning, BEFORE you read the paper, watch TV, or drive to work. In other words, before the 'negative' team get to work.

They need to be written out about five times a week, ie daily. They should then be read aloud.

95% of people can't be bothered with this sort of thing – only 5% or less have a success mentality. I think that is a rotten shame – just be sure you are in the 5%. Scepticism is rampant.

However, by applying these techniques, I pulled myself out of a situation of being £10,000 in debt with no assets and no job, to owning a business operating in three countries and having a reasonable income and a good lifestyle.

Setting Goals For Networking

How on earth do you do this? As with anything, decide what you want.

1. X number of Referrals
2. X amount of new contacts
3. X amount of cash as a profit for the time
   and money invested

Then work out how many events you need to attend, how many new contacts you need to make, how much time you plan to allocate etc.

Now, set it out in chronological order, set a date, make the goals a bit hard, i.e. stretch. Write them out over and over on a daily basis. As you achieve a goal, celebrate, re-set your goals – adding a new one!

Never have more than ten goals, or the mind loses focus. Have some short term goals, medium and long term – but ALWAYS write a date.

The great thing is you are never wrong. It is between you and you – no one else.

You can change, reset, scrap one altogether. Without goals, unfortunately, that is what you achieve – not much.

Without goals, unfortunately, that is what you achieve – not much

Imagine starting a journey to a town you don't know, in a district with which you are not familiar. By just setting out – how long will the journey take? Ridiculous, isn't it? So is running your life without a map. I know, I did it for a long time!

It is exactly the same with networking. It is possible to set a goal to earn £25,000 profit from a networked activity. Set the goal and see for yourself.

Gearing Up!

Be prepared to deal with so much new business.

Reader, if you implement a plan to get new business through word of mouth recommendation you need to understand that success will bring in more business than you bargained for.

BNI is now five years old in the UK. We have seen many instances where a continuous stream of referrals has meant serious growth for the company involved. A fencing contractor grew from three employees to twenty three on the back of his "chapter" referring him business. An electrician developed a business with six employees, where previously he had only a van and himself. This growing business was then able to tackle "new build" projects.

Some people are afraid of growth. Some people are self-employed but actually have a "job" – in so much as they are too indispensable – can't take a day off. Only have a week's holiday. They should read Robert Kiyosaki's "Cash Flow Quadrant".

Getting a stream of referred business is the way off a treadmill for some people – be prepared to go to a new level – join a referral organisation so that you can count on a stream of new business over a period of time stretching into years.

ᴵ◀◀

Getting a stream of referred business is the way off a treadmill for some people

This group could easily become your biggest customer – treat them with respect, and "learn the ropes" quickly.

Be Prepared To Meet Finance Requirements

Receiving larger orders or contracts than you are accustomed to means you need to be a good budget manager.

Larger contracts require larger cash injection. It is obvious but some companies do not gear themselves to finance sufficiently, then let down clients AND... the referrer. This leads to frustration and fewer referrals.

Be aware that growing the company needs good management, and tight controls.

Staffing To The Right Level

How much extra manpower will be required and can this be sustained? This is a difficult area, but a well structured referral organisation is a very secure source of new business, and is easy to maintain and sustain.

PART II

THE COMPLETE NETWORKER

by Andrew Hall

www.HandyGuides.net

Chapter One

SPEAK IN PUBLIC?
YOU MUST BE JOKING!

It's late. The evening meeting ran over far too long and now you face the long drive home. Rain lashes the windscreen, ageing wipers affording only a moments respite each time they pass. Desperately tired, you struggle through the gloom in front.

Suddenly, without warning, the road veers sharply right. Slow reactions are no match for such an unexpected turn. Your car leaves the road, the sodden ground taking possession of the vehicle that is now hurtling downwards. A deafening roar of sound announces the end of the mudslide - and the arrival of water. A strange silence ensues as the car at first sits upon the lake, but then slowly starts to submerge. You struggle with the door, but the weight of water seals you in. Electric windows offer no comfort now. Gradually at first, then quickening, the car fills with water.

Drowning is perhaps one of the most vivid and real fears that can grip our imagination. We can all picture it, all imagine the absolute panic that choking would bring. But asked to list the most potent fear in our minds, it is not one we would choose. Indeed, asked to select their greatest fear, respondents do not opt for the terrifying death by drowning; not the choking asphyxiation of a smoke filled room; not even the cold, lonely, slow death from a mountain fall. For most people their greatest and most relevant fear is no more than the fear of Public Speaking.

There is nothing quite so frightening as being asked to speak in public. Recently, Robert and I have been working to establish BNI in Malaysia. On our first trip, we decided to assess the local networking groups and potential competition, and found ourselves at the BNC (Business Networking Club). Assembled there were many of the great businessmen and women who were to provide the backbone of BNI's subsequent development. But that is not my abiding memory of the evening. For there were 48 business owners in the room, to a man there for one purpose – to grow their business through networking. A microphone was placed in the middle and offered to anybody who wanted to promote his business.

Just two people stood – Robert and I

The prospect of speaking before an audience, with the certain knowledge that all are giving you their full attention – watching you, judging you – is enough to induce total paralysis into otherwise dynamic business owners. Yet the rewards in social and particularly in business life from being able to communicate to as large an audience as possible are immense. Winston Churchill, one of the greatest orators in history, knew from an early age of the influence to be gained from becoming an able speaker. Lord Chatham, who led England to victory in the Seven Year's War, convinced Churchill that oratory gave its possessor "A power more durable than that of a Great king" (Churchill I).

◀◀

"A power more durable than that of a Great king"

As it was for Churchill, so it is for us in business. In one of the first groups I launched for BNI, a double-glazing salesman joined the group. Typical of his trade, speaking one on one, he was confident, brash, and articulate. Yet, when he rose to speak before the group, he changed – he would stutter, lose his way, return to the start of his talk. It was painful to watch.

When we launched the group, 120 people were in the room, and my fingers were crossed as he rose to speak, willing him to get through his one-minute presentation.

My reason for telling this story is that I came back to the Chapter a couple of months later, and this man was giving his ten minute talk. Only now he was different. Gone was the hesitant, mumbling speaker I had nursed through his early presentations, and in its place was the lively, assertive individual I had met at the start. Speaking to him afterwards, he told me that he had actually turned down being the best man at a close friends wedding in the past simply because he could not face the subsequent speech. There is so much to be gained in so many areas of life, if we are able to speak in public.

They say that the key to a great game of golf is to take a lesson before you ever swing a club, and then practice, practice, practice. Richard Branson, surely one of the most confident people you could imagine, shunned public speaking for much of his early life. Just 18, he set up his first magazine, "Student", from a phone box at his public school. Seemingly without fear, he called many of the greatest companies in the land and persuaded them to advertise. The first edition read like a "Who's Who" of the great and the good from the day – and with sound reason. Branson got hold of a copy and set about contacting as many of its entries as he could. Peter Blake (artist for the Beatles Sgt Pepper album), Vanessa Redgrave, David Hockney, John Le Carre and many more all contributing, simply because a brash 18 year old had the courage to ask.

But, surprisingly, this same man has never been a confident public speaker, and if you wished to find the cause of this anomaly, you need look no further than one of his earliest attempts. Thrown into the spotlight, under the glare of German television and a mass of excited students and activists at a rally

So much to be gained if we are able to speak in public

outside University College London, Branson froze, and his speech collapsed into a desperate ramble. He fled from the stage.

Such false starts can easily handicap a speaker for life. Luckily, for the committed networker today, there are many opportunities to ease your way into the world of confident, effective speech making. Groups such as Toastmasters, BNI, and the multitude of regular networking meetings, afford the opportunity to hone and develop your skills in readiness to grab any chance to put your business in front of and above many others. Here are the secrets that I have learned that will ensure success every time you to stand up to speak...

Be Prepared

"That is the resolve of his Majesty's Government – every man of them. That is the will of Parliament and the nation. The British Empire and the French Republic, linked together in their cause and in their need, will defend to their death their native soil, aiding each other like good comrades to the utmost of their strength. Even though large tracts of Europe and many old and famous States have fallen or may fall into the grip of the Gestapo and all the odious apparatus of Nazi rule, we shall not flag or fail. We shall go on to the end, we shall fight in France, we shall fight on the seas and the oceans, we shall fight with growing confidence and growing strength in the air, we shall defend our island, whatever the cost may be, we shall fight on the beaches, we shall fight on the landing grounds, we shall fight on the fields and in the streets, we shall fight in the hills; we shall never surrender...

Crafted words that roused the House of Commons to a thunderous ovation

The words, of course, of Winston Churchill. Delivered not after a famous victory, but rather the miraculous avoidance of disaster at Dunkirk. Words that inspired a nation. Crafted words that roused the House of Commons to a thunderous ovation. And above all else, words that delivered what Churchill wanted most – American military aid to Britain. For they convinced the U.S. President Roosevelt that "As long as that old bastard is in charge, Britain will never surrender!"

Strange to think that the man capable of delivering a speech acknowledged at the time by the author Harold Nicholson as the "most magnificent words ever heard in the English Language", was born with a speech impediment that left him incapable of pronouncing the letter "s". Curious also to think that his early efforts offered little clue to the great speaker who was to emerge. So sharp in general conversation, Churchill was rendered almost helpless with anxiety at the prospect of public speaking. As he readily admitted, "For many years I was unable to say anything I had not written out and committed to memory beforehand."

What made the difference with this, perhaps the first "Professional" politician, was an understanding of the unbending need to be prepared. Such historic lines did not simply fall from his lips. Session after session, standing in front of the mirror running through old speeches he had committed to memory honed his skill. His friend, the lawyer FE Smith, once jealously remarked, "Winston spent much of his life preparing for his impromptu speeches", but Churchill consoled himself with the knowledge that "Rhetorical power

◄◄

"Winston spent much of his life preparing for his impromptu speeches"

is neither wholly bestowed, nor wholly acquired, but cultivated." His Butler soon became familiar with his commitment. "As soon as he got into the bath he would start muttering. At first I thought he was talking to me. I said, "Do you want me?"
"I wasn't talking to you, Norman." He replied, "I was addressing the House of Commons!"

Great orators command the attention of all before them, and to the committed networker, effective speaking assures the widest possible audience to your services. The first time I truly became aware of the power of great speechmaking came not in business nor indeed from politics, but in 1985, dragged along to a rock concert to see an artist I knew little of and cared even less. As the rain poured down upon the St James Park stadium in Newcastle, and Bruce Springsteen launched into tracks of little consequence to me, I was sure I had made a huge mistake.

Until he paused to speak

For he spoke with a passion and conviction that held and seized his audience, and left a mark on all who heard him. Public speaking, like any concert or play, is a live performance, and to engross and hold the attention of your audience, should have a "Live" feel. Your audience should never quite relax, never be quite sure where you are going next. There is no shortcut to giving such a feeling. Whether you are a politician, showman, or a networking speechmaker, you have got to be Prepared. Richard Nixon, always a master in public persuasion, summed it best, when he confirmed: "No performance takes such special preparation as an off-the-cuff talk."

|◄◄

"No ...performance takes such special preparation as an off-the-cuff talk"

The Words

Monumental events like Second World War or Watergate are of such magnitude, and the attention of the audience to every line so assured, that there is a very real sense that the words do not really matter. Even badly put, the message would have got across. Unfortunately, for most of us in business, our topics are not in themselves of immediate massive interest to our listeners. We can all remember from our school days, sleeping through lessons that seemed of little relevance. Yet, just as clearly, we can probably remember the class or teacher who, given a similar subject, held our attention and became a source of inspiration. The difference, so often, is in the words.

For every speech, I start by gathering all of the points that I wish to get across, and placing them in a logical, flowing order. This form gives structure to the speech and will also help me later when I come to deliver it. But this is only the beginning and from this point on, all of my work is aimed at carrying my audience with me, so that they will soak up the information and be inspired to put it into action.

Advertisers have known for years that stories captivate an audience, and that if they note the story, they stand a better chance of remembering the product. One of the most successful campaigns in the U.K. in recent years was for Nescafe™ Gold Blend™. The idea was simple. Two people meeting through a succession of ads as a romance slowly came to the boil. The viewing public was soon hooked, eagerly awaiting each new episode. Articles were written in Newspapers and Magazines, the actors became celebrities, and along the way, a product was taken from obscurity to become perhaps the most famous premium brand of instant coffee in Britain.

Successful public speaking follows all of these rules. For each point I deliver, there is a story to back it up. A story that may bear no direct relation to the subject – its relevance lying in the message it carries alongside. For the most powerful messages to reinforce a point are rarely cold statistics or cases, but relevant diversions drawn from the well of your life experience.

For example, if I am trying to explain that you can never be too prepared, I might use a story thus:

"Rolls Royce recently sold for $479m to Volkswagen. I have no doubt that Volkswagen did their due diligence and considered themselves well prepared. But it was around two weeks later that the news started to filter out that:

"Yes", they had bought the factory,

"Yes" they had bought the right to produce the car, BUT they had FAILED to acquire the most valuable part of all – the name. And from here on Volkswagen will have to produce Bentleys. You can never be too prepared."

Interesting stories like this hold an audience, so that an important issue that may have gone un-noted or ignored (In this case "You can never be too prepared") has now been absorbed by everyone in the room.

The Delivery

Relevant stories help to give your speech a vibrant feel. But to carry an audience through a ten, thirty, or sixty-minute presentation requires more – and the secret is found in the delivery of the material itself. Textbook advice on speechmaking usually confines itself to "Keep your head high and look them straight in the eye" and indeed this is important. I recently held a business meeting with a contact who was seeking my help. But throughout his pitch to me, his eyes rarely left the security of the business partner he had with him. His distance left me disinclined to help, and disinterested in what he had to say. Strong firm eye contact with as many in the room as you can throughout your speech will greatly assist in holding the attention of your audience. But if you want them hanging onto your every word, you need to do a little more.

⏮ *Looking straight in their eyes is only the beginning*

When I was young, I attended a local comprehensive school. The lottery of class allocation threw me into perhaps the worst group of the year, rubbing shoulders with 30 others, whose prime goal seemed to be to get through the next few years learning as little as possible, the associated frustrations of which to be vented on **all** in authority. All that is, except one man – a biology teacher who on the face of it had much to fear from a class such as mine. For he was a short man, with a seemingly mild manner. But it was his approach that assured him control over every situation. He would always enter the class late, walking into a cacophony of noise, 30 kids talking about girls/ boys, holidays, the latest music – in fact everything bar Biology. He would say nothing, but had with him a four-foot ruler. Still without a word, he would raise the rule above his head before bringing it crashing down upon the desk.

Silence...

What he had done was to take a group of individuals with little or no interest in him or his subject, and said "Hey! Listen to me." And a great speech does exactly the same. Be it through a stunt (the crashing ruler) or the opposite (10 seconds of silence can be so strong), through a great story well told, or simply through the energy with which you rise to the stage, from the moment you begin, your audience should be shaken out of the comfortable malaise of their rest as you say "Hey! Listen to me" – a dynamic, prepared speaker has risen to his feet and you do not want to miss a word.

Asked to pick out one fundamental difference between good speakers and great ones, for me there is no question – great talkers **leave their notes behind**. Only then will a presentation take on the true conversational style that is so enthralling. A few years ago in the U.K., a rather unlikely politician shot to prominence in the Conservative Party. Ann Widdecombe on the face of it has none of the attributes required by today's "Makeover" politicians – plain looks and a rather squeaky voice are scarcely ideal assets for the ambitious politician. But her moment came at the party conference in 1998. Rising to speak, she passed by the speakers podium, forwent the autocue beloved of the modern leader, and stepped down towards the audience to deliver a speech of convincing passion, rich in relevant stories, jokes and anecdotes, all flowing seemingly "from the hip". A conference star was born.

As ever, the secret to such a free flowing, "Impromptu" speech is in reality full preparation. Great speechmakers never stand without knowing in their mind exactly where they are going with their talk. Understand that every time your eyes cut to you notes, your audience starts to drift away. The truly "Live" feel is lost, replaced with the sense that you have a succession of points to get through and your speech becomes something to be endured rather than enjoyed. No magician, comedian, or actor would ever stand up with notes in hand - and for very good reason.

◄◄

Great Public Speakers carry no notes

In such a speech, it follows that there is also no place for the crutch of modern day speechmaking – the standard PowerPoint™ Presentation. Nothing is more likely to induce sleep among your audience than the sight of page after page of bullet pointed screens. Through my time at Cambridge, it seemed that every dull lecturer also produced a "Flyer" to accompany his talk. Pretty soon, students got wise, and the start of his talk would see a stream of undergraduates arrive, collect the notes, only to beat a hasty retreat back to their rooms. Flyers or bullet pointed screens remove the feeling of originality in a speech, and disengage the audience. In a "Live" speech, PowerPoint™ is a prop, brought out at key moments with a **picture** or **chart** to dramatically bolster your message while distracting no one from the talk itself.

Indeed, a confident delivery will include a copious amount of different but relevant props. All the while you have something in your hand, you can be sure that you have everyone's attention.

We can all remember as children visiting a local magic show and being enthralled as the magician enchanted us with trick after trick. The words helped, but it was the props that ensured our eyes never strayed far from his act. We may be older now, but the rules for holding an audience are just the same. Items relevant to your business, be they examples of your work, like publications for the printer, or products, such as laptops or peripherals

Powerpoint™ is a prop – and nothing else

for the computer supplier, both hold our attention while confirming the skill and depth of knowledge you retain in your business.

But perhaps the most powerful props of all are those that have nothing to do with the subject at all.

Four years ago, I visited a networking group in the Midlands and witnessed one of the most effective presentations I have yet seen. The solicitor had just one minute to get his message across, and as he rose he placed on the table in front of him a plinth. From his case, he then drew out an egg, which was then placed on the plinth. Finally, from under the table he raised a huge mallet, which he held menacingly above the egg. His fellow members were nervous now! The room rustled to the sound of those unfortunate enough to be sitting near, drawing away from the firing line. But to their great surprise, he proceeded to talk about his business for one minute, the services he offered and the clients he was particularly seeking. As his minute came to a close, he rounded off "John Quinney, solicitor", and sat down. Everyone looked aghast. The members on his table, breathing slightly easier now, finally plucked up the courage to ask, "So what's with the egg, John?". John Quinney rose to his feet once more and revealed:

"I just wanted to make sure that I had your full attention!"

My point in telling you this story is that four years on, I can remember his name. There is not one other person in the room that morning that I could name or probably even remember.

Both John Quinney and the magician knew the power of interacting with their audience, and you should do so too. Even with nothing to show, you can keep your audience on its toes through the simple act of movement. I remember as a child my first trip to the circus. Clowns bounded around the stage and then, without warning, would rush into the audience to select another "Victim" to pull into the ring. I was both enthralled and terrified. But every ounce of my concentration was focussed on the act.

I was both enthralled and terrified...

Nothing galvanises attention quite like the knowledge that at any moment you could be in the spotlight, and your "Live performance" should bring with it that tension. Move close to your audience if you can, and then away, threaten to invade their private space, and every message you wish to deliver will fall onto attentive ears.

Avoiding The Big Freeze

"Who Am I? Why Am I Here?"

The only words no lesser man than Admiral Stockdale could conjure when "Freezing" during the U.S. Vice Presidential debate in 1992 in front of 100 million American viewers. Fear of "The Big Freeze" is the one thing that keeps most people rooted to their seats when the opportunity to shine in a presentation presents itself. Leslie Howard was a famous stage actor at the turn of the century and made a name for himself by appearing in several different plays on the same day. One night, every actor's nightmare struck Howard – he forgot his next line. He froze and waited meekly for the "prompt" behind the curtain. Nothing came. Howard

moved around the stage, trying to look purposeful –
still nothing. Finally, in desperation he hissed,
"Which line?" From the shadows returned an
equally desperate voice:

◄◄

Leave the fear of

drying up to others

"Which play?!"

Fortunately, for the public speaker no one knows
the next line but you, and no one will know if the
line you give is not correct. Indeed, whenever I
stand to speak, I do so armed with a few little tricks
that leave the "Fear of drying up" to others.

As always, preparation is the key, and critically if
the stage is to be your friend and not your foe, you
need to know your surroundings. Tom O'Connor
tells a wonderful story about the keen amateur
actor, given his first stage role. He has just one line:
"Hark! I hear the cannons roar". Day and night he
rehearses for his big chance. As soon as he wakes:
"Hark! I hear the cannons roar", in the shower
"Hark! I hear the cannons roar", on the bus,
watching TV, in bed, "Hark! I hear the cannons roar".
No one could be more prepared. Come the first
night, our actor stands confidently awaiting his cue.

Just as the moment arrives, the stage manager gives the signal for a sound effect and there is a deafening bang from backstage. And our actor says: "Bloody Hell! What was that?"

For the public speaker, knowledge of your surroundings means: Never stand to speak without having already stood on the stage or spot from where you will present. It is amazing how disorientating it is to leap up from the audience and turn to face them, just at the moment when your blood is running fast. Muhammad Ali accredits many of his first round knockouts to the "Freezing" of his opponents, scared not of him, but bewildered by the environment. He would engineer it so that he was always first to enter the ring; he would check the feel of the canvas underfoot so that his feet would be secure as he danced around; he would check the tension of the ropes so that he knew how far he could lean on them to evade the early blows; and most importantly of all, he would get comfortable with the audience – the excited faces of thousands of expectant fight fans. At moments of stress, your environment needs to be familiar and comfortable to you if you are to avoid freezing with

⏮
Muhammad Ali has so much to teach the great public speaker

fear. I never stand to speak without first having stood on the stage or podium from where I will present, and looked out over the rows of seats. I cut the "bloodrush" by standing as soon as my introduction begins and moving to the side of the stage. This gets me to my feet, and comfortable with looking out at my audience, before I rise to the stage. I reduce it further by visualising myself leaping onto the stage and launching into a dynamic, successful delivery.

You will see that the key to avoiding the big freeze lies in being comfortable with your surroundings and secure in your thoughts. If things are going to go wrong, they will usually do so at the beginning. Knowing this, I always have the first three minutes taped – rehearsed to the point where I could deliver them whatever my state of mind. Perversely, from then on the only real danger of freezing comes if ever the thought of drying up enters your head. For the novice speaker, such thoughts herald an almost immediate paralysis as their thought processes grind to a halt. It is very much like when you were a child and were walking into the living room with a cup and

⏮ **Familiarity keeps you calm**

saucer. All was going well until your worried parents said: "Don't spill that drink", and suddenly you became a helpless butterfingers, and an accident was assured.

Again, the solution lies in being prepared and in familiarity with whatever may hit us. Ali shows us the way here once more. He trained himself to recognise when he had been knocked cold and actually went into an "Autopilot" routine he likened to entering a strange room, a room full of neon orange and green lights that he called "The Half Dream Room." Familiarity with this room and its passing effect allowed him to recognise it when it happened, remain standing and protect himself while his brain recovered. Recalling his infamous "Rumble in the Jungle" fight with World Heavyweight Champion, the fearsome George Foreman in 1974, Ali acknowledges being knocked senseless twice in round two without the other fighter recognising that victory was his for the taking. In the eighth round, Ali finally knocked his man over, and most observers were surprised that the champion did not get up in time. But, as Ali explained, Foreman was an undefeated champion – he had never been in the "Half Dream" room before.

If Muhammad Ali can conceal being knocked cold with the whole world watching, we, in our speeches, can surely conceal a lapse of memory. Picture the scene. You are on the podium, a thousand people enjoying your great presentation, when suddenly it happens, your mind goes blank. You freeze, helpless on the stage. Every speakers worst nightmare. But wait a minute. What if you had a simple get out line, there for you to draw on if ever such a situation arose? For the last three years, I have carried the following joke in my armoury – a comfort whose simple presence somehow ensures I never need it:

⏮
You freeze, helpless on the stage...

"Do you know, for a moment there I completely blacked out. I forgot totally what I was saying. I felt a bit like the nervous speaker who stood before his audience and said, "When I got up this morning only my wife and I knew what I was going to speak about. Now only my wife knows!"

Your audience will roar with laughter, be certain that you are so assured as a speaker that you put the line in only to tell the joke, and you will have bought yourself the short time you need for your brain to return to you.

"There are three points you need to consider..."
Why did I ever say those words in front of local networking group as I gave a short presentation? My last piece of advice to the "Live" speaker is to never enumerate your points. True to the child with the cup and saucer, my brain took the third point, locked it in a box, there to be held until my presentation was over. Strange to think that, just as with that child, without the prior numerical statement, all of my three points would have remained firmly in mind. With familiarity, preparation, and an understanding of the very few pitfalls that actually face the focussed public speaker, the fear of freezing really can be left to the rest.

And Finally!

If there is a secret to successful presenting, it lies in full preparation. I recently heard a speaker claim that for every minute she spoke, she spent one hour preparing, and I believe that is the key.

For the rewards for such investment are huge. The able speaker has at his disposal perhaps the most powerful tool of the complete networker – **the ability to move an entire audience to his cause**. One of my abiding memories from my schooldays is of a maths lesson when I was 14. I was just quietly drifting away, gazing out of the window, when suddenly I heard my name, as the teacher demanded an answer from me to a question that I had not heard. For a long time, I blamed my poor concentration. But today, I have the consolation that my teacher simply did not know how to hold his audience!

Chapter Two

THE FIRST IMPRESSION

"I am an Accountant... There is not a lot more I can say really."

Thus began the membership in BNI of one of the founding members of my first group. Asked to present for sixty seconds, Tony delivered just fourteen words before he sat down. We all laughed, Tony returned to his seat and the meeting moved on.

But, damage had been done. Looking back on it today, it is clear to me that this was also the moment where Tony's membership floundered. For an image had been set in all of our minds. Tony was the stereotypical accountant (CPA). Not a trusted business adviser and dynamic manipulator of figures, but a dull, boring clone of the kind lampooned by Monty Python and comedians everywhere. It would not be possible to refer Tony.

The tragedy in those early words was that the reality was so different. In the years that have followed I have heard great testimonies to his work – his tremendous ability to save his clients tax, his tenacious competence in handling government investigations. But you never get a second chance to make a first impression. 14 ill-judged words and a die had been cast. Within a year, Tony was gone.

You never get a second chance to make a first impression

One of the fruits of active networking is that you will find yourself thrown, almost daily in front of new business contacts. Faced with such abundance, the very real danger is that you lose sight of the huge potential sitting right under your nose – the daily flow of new business contacts, and thus pay little mind to perhaps the most significant factor in your future relationship: Their first impression. The economic recession in the UK through the 1990's brought many building companies to their knees. One of those caught up in the crisis was a company local to me in Sussex, England. A family firm, handed down through the generations for over a century. As the property market crashed around him, the present owner, the Great Grandson of the founder, did everything in his power to save the family business. Finally, overwhelmed by debts of £250,000, the receivers moved in.

As the accountants poured over the books, a repeated ledger caught their eye – regular purchases of coal made by the firm, unusual for a company in the building trade. Upon their next visit, enquiries were made, and the receiver was taken to a back room where an old steam engine stood, furnishing the power that drove all of the tools in the workshop. You can see that steam engine today. It was sold by the receiver to our National Museum for over £500,000. All along, the very key to the company's salvation rested right under the owner's nose.

The truth is that you have no idea of the business opportunities that lie behind each new contact you meet. Just before the turn of the twentieth century,

◀◀

You have no idea of the business potential behind each new contact you meet

an elderly couple entered a hotel lobby and asked for a room. It was a stormy night and there was a delegation in town. The clerk apologised, for he was full. What is more, he explained that they would have great difficulty finding a room anywhere that night. But as he watched the old couple turn out into the night, the clerk called them back. "I cannot let you go back out into this weather", he said, "Why don't you take my room?" The elderly couple accepted the kind offer and when the old man came down to pay his bill the next morning, he spoke of his gratitude. "You are just the kind of person I would like to have working with me. Give me your card. Maybe someday I will build a hotel for you to run."

It was some four years later that an air ticket arrived, inviting the clerk to travel to New York to meet once more with the old man. He found himself standing at the corner of Fifth Avenue and Thirty Fourth Street, in front of a huge, fabulous new building. "This is the hotel I have built for you to run", the old man explained. His name was William Waldorf-Astor. The hotel was the first Waldorf Astoria and the clerk who accepted the first managerial position was George C Boldt.

Such events, when they appear in the "Real World" become noted, regaled in magazines and books such as this. But in networking, similar opportunities are being seized (and spurned) every single day. Here in my home area of Sussex I have witnessed, in the last month, a BNI member pull his biggest client, a multi National Corporation, through a visitor who came just the once. I have witnessed an accountant, locked out from membership by an associate, pass over £90,000 in business to a member he had just met. Common to all of these examples was the strength of the first impression. In any meeting between two strangers, you can be certain that one of the first questions posed will be "What do you do?" How you answer, can have important repercussions on your financial future.

Ask any number of business people "What do you do" and almost to a man they will fall back on the easy, stock answer. "I am an accountant (CPA)"; "I am a travel agent." But in doing so, they are closing a door – a door to potential business that they had only just opened. The major corporations have much to teach us here. Break it down and MacDonald's™ sell hamburgers, Nike sell what were called in my school

In Networking huge deals from chance meetings are a daily event

days, training shoes. But you will never catch either of them talking about their products in such terms – and neither should you in your business. Come across either of these products and you will find companies in complete control of your entire experience. Buy a bottle of Coca Cola™ and nothing is left to chance. The fridge will in all likelihood have been provided, smothered with attractive promotional material. The bottle is not simple and functional but sculpted, giving a very emotional element to the purchase of flavoured sugar water.

The serious businessman is never "just an Accountant", or "just a Travel Agent." It follows that his introduction should be a definite statement of benefits for his operation, a gateway inviting further enquiries – and thus business opportunities.

Recently, I was invited to a large networking event in Sussex and chanced upon an "Accountant". I knew this was his trade as the name badge he had been given described him as such. But when I dropped the "What do you do?" line, his response surprised me. For he said: "You know those companies that have been growing quickly and have the capacity plus the

The large corporations have much to teach us on getting noticed

ambition to grow further. Firms such as . . ." he rattled off three local firms that I would know and to whom I would relate. "I guide them through to the next stage. I structure the company with an eye on the future, to minimise the tax liability of both the company and all of the directors involved."

I had known him for less than a minute, but from my first impression, I wanted him as my accountant. Here was a man who knew his business, and knew exactly who he wanted to do business with. Chatting to him later, I found out of course that he also did general accounts, but here was his passion. I also found out that the three companies he had listed were not clients, they were targets. If I had responded that I knew one intimately, he would have worked himself onto the brink of a referral.

⏮ **Memory Hooks are at the heart of corporate branding – it should be no different for your business**

Transferred to a weekly networking meeting, the ability to introduce yourself with impact extends beyond greeting the latest visitors and into your very presentation itself. Here again, we can learn from the large corporate companies. Hear the words "The Best a Man Can Get!" and you know I am talking of Gillette™. The mere mention of Nike™

calls the words "Just Do it"™ to trip off the tongue. These are **Memory Hooks** – simple lines that accompany every piece of advertising or promotion for a company, and become intrinsically linked in our minds with the product.

For the large corporations that dominate our retail markets, a substantial part of their capital is not physical, but the value of their brand recognition, manifest in their memory hooks. At a recent shareholder meeting, the boss of Coca Cola™ was able to proclaim that even if every manufacturing plant in his company was destroyed overnight, the value of Coca Cola™ would still be some $150bn – because of the value of its trademarks.

It is easy to conclude that the creation of such a potent corporate identity is the sole preserve of the largest companies. But if a company such as Coca Cola™ can generate in its trademarks alone a value greater than all of its physical capital, just imagine the potential for your own business, in your local market, from creating a single identity associated by all who see or hear it with your product or service, for it runs throughout every piece of promotional work

MEMORY HOOKS

"If Spectrum put it in, you can put it out"
Ben Crease,
Spectrum Fire Services

"When your spine's in line, you'll feel fine"
Jeremy Spanton,
Chiropractor

"Your inky fingered printer"
Betty Harrison, Printer

you do. The Nike hook and logo is perhaps the most famous in the world today. But all companies start somewhere, even Nike. Their hook began life in a student's college room, sold on for just $35.

There is no better place to begin than your weekly network meeting. With every presentation you give, the flourish at its close should be your memory hook. Develop a line for your business that is sharp, memorable, and destined to be forever associated with your product or service. It should never be changed. As time goes by, you will almost certainly come up with new and better lines, but your loyalty to the first should be set in stone.

Coca Cola's™ hook is "The Real Thing"™™. Launched at the time when the opening shots of the Cola wars with Pepsi™ were being fired, "The Real Thing"™™ probably made sense. But in today's world, it is hard to imagine an advertising executive standing before the chief executive of Coca Cola ™ and proclaiming "We are going to take your sleek bottle with its secret recipe and identify it with a 1970's pop group!" Strange to think then that today "The Real Thing"™™ is probably the most valuable trademark in the world. Its

⏮

MEMORY HOOKS
"The future's bright, the future's green, the future's Evergreen
Gary Chapman,
Evergreen Letting Agents

"For a first impression that is worth a second look"
Mark Keatley-Palmer,
Sycamore Design

"Making your money work harder than you do"
Alan Jackson,
Financial Advisor

value lies in the fact that it has never been changed – and neither should yours.

Used at every network event you attend, a good memory hook will lodge in the minds of each contact you meet. But this is only the beginning, for your hook line should never be left behind at the door of your network meeting. My belief is that your memory hook should be on your business card; letterhead; it should be on the sign over your door; and it should form part of every piece of advertising that you do.

As an active networker, you are going to present before at least 1,000 business people in the coming year. But memories are short, and within a matter of days most will have forgotten your name. But they will remember your hook. If in the days that follow, they see your trademark on the sign over your premises, they will identify with you from that moment on. Or perhaps a year later, they are finally in the market for your product or services. Long since having forgotten meeting you, they reach for the Yellow Pages. Your advert sits lost among 300 in your line of work, until they notice your strap line, and the lights come on. Yours will be the number they call.

MEMORY HOOKS

"Don't cook the books, book the Cook!"
Robert Cook,
Platinum Financial Services

"Making you look good on paper"
Des Booth, Prontaprint

"Vinyl Design - the name that sticks"
Steve Jones, Sign Writer

With a good Hook, every meeting sows a seed that may bear fruit at any time in the future

Recently, on a trip to Malaysia, I met a lady who had put it all together. She was "An Accountant", and her trademark caught my eye "The Messier the Better". It was on her card, letterhead, and the basis for all of her promotional work. I was intrigued. "Why 'the Messier the Better'?" I asked. As she replied, I could see it was a question she was used to:

"Most of us, when we start in business pay little mind to our accounts. There is simply far too much to do launching a company from scratch. Time passes quickly, receipts pile up in carrier bags and soon we become aware that we really should have taken more care with our records. Embarrassed, we are scared to pick up the phone. This is my market. New, fast moving companies – the businesses of the future. "The Messier the Better" puts them at their ease, and mine is the number they call."

First impressions count. Careful attention to both the way you introduce yourself to every new contact, and to building a consistent trademark through all of your promotional activity, will lock your business with credibility in the minds of all you meet. A powerful trademark such as "The Messier the Better" stands on its own. For most of us, delivering such a line is a new experience, and I know from the groups I attend, there is a strong temptation to warn in advance of its arrival, to state "My memory hook is…" But just remember, Coca Cola™, MacDonald's™, and Nike™ do not say: "My memory hook is." In fact Nike don't say anything at all. So strong is their hook line today that all they need to is draw the swoosh logo, and our minds as one deliver the message: "Just do it!"

Chapter Three

CHOOSING YOUR NEXT CUSTOMER

Consider for a moment the vast array of clients and companies that comprise the customer database for your company. Think further, and focus upon just how these clients have arrived at your door. For most of us in business, our stock of clients is drawn not from a single source, but from a multitude of avenues as we exploit every opportunity open to us for fresh business.

I remember very well the start of my first business. Fresh from University, I began an art dealing business. With no experience to draw from, I attacked every opening with equal vigour – I sent out fliers, placed advertisements both locally and nationally, made cold calls, liaised with galleries, and slowly assembled the motley collection of individuals who comprised my early clients.

So much activity, so many sources for new business. But if I had to pick out one unifying factor through them all, it would be this. I had very little influence let alone control over the outcomes. It was as if I was a passenger on a roller coaster ride where the margins between success and failure were small indeed. I remember working through the night to produce a 30,000 leaflet mail shot. The result? Just one client – a disastrous failure and I vowed never to do such a thing again. But within six months as this one client went on to finance my first Gallery and catapulted a small local business into the London Arena, things looked very different. Success or failure hanging by a knife- edge – business reality for so many small and medium sized companies.

Being part of an organised, structured referral organisation gives you, perhaps for the first time, a direct hand in the clients and customers that you take on. For you find yourself in league with a mass of like-minded business owners and proprietors, to a man willing to help those prepared to assist them in return. And for a brief moment each week, the room is silent; the stage is yours..

...and you can ask for anything you want

My role in this chapter is to give you the tools that you need to secure for your own business precisely the referrals that you are seeking – to quite literally "Choose Your Next Customer". Like so many of the opportunities that present themselves in life, it is so easy in the excitement and immediacy of presenting for perhaps just a minute, to let the potential pass you by – to simply wash over you. Winston Churchill warned many decades ago: "Men occasionally stumble over the truth but most pick themselves up and hurry off as if nothing has happened". To an outsider, it will not be clear which path you have trod. In both cases you will have spoken when asked, and contributed where required. But the answer will scream in the results you achieve.

A year or so ago, travelling to one of my networking groups in Surrey, I met a member who approached

⏮

"Men occasionally stumble over the truth, but most pick themselves up and hurry off as if nothing has happened"

me full of excitement. He was drawing so much business from the organisation; his only challenge was finding enough to pass back in gratitude to the other members in his group. His business was "Fire Protection". It was just two days later that I paid a call to one of our largest groups and found there a long-standing member, about to announce that he was to leave the group. He had given it his best, been regular in his attendance, but was disappointed to have never really made the breakthrough into third party referrals. His business?

Fire protection!

Two members, the same business, but a total contrast in the results achieved.

The seeds of such disparity of achievement are often sown even before a foot is stepped inside the networking arena. My experience has shown me that top performers carry with them a belief in the certainty of their success, that flows through every action they take. Running art Galleries gave me the opportunity to meet some of the U.K.'s top business entrepreneurs. One who sticks in my mind was

Maurice Saatchi. I recall travelling to his home in Sussex. Dressed in a simple gown and slippers, he took me out to show me around the lake he had built. But my mind could not focus on the scene. For as this mild, kindly, unassuming man led me around, one question screamed in my head - "How did such a man manage in just a few short years to put together the largest advertising agency in the world."

What I discovered of course, was that Saatchi possessed what I believe is true of all top performers, and certainly all top networkers – a certainty of belief in their ultimate success. It would have been so easy for the Saatchi's to assume that all of the top advertising clients – Proctor and Gamble, British Airways etc - were taken and beyond the grasp of a newcomer onto the scene. But Saatchi had belief, and would ring each with an intriguing offer. "We have been looking at your advertising campaigns and feel that we can improve them yet further. What is more, we have invested several weeks putting together an advertising proposition for you. Can we come around and show it to you?" No such work had been done of course, and any "Yes" would be a

Your network represents a sales force for your business

starting gun for a period of frantic activity from the design team to come up with a campaign from scratch before the imminent appointment.

Top networkers match Saatchi's belief because they know that so often in life, it is your expectation that drives the result. I remember the arrival of Marcus Emery into one of my groups. He had a pretty unique business, owning the largest warehouse in the region. Of more concern when he joined, he owned the largest empty warehouse in the region, having just lost his biggest client. Marcus was hungry and focussed. He had no hope of "Internal" business – none of his members had use for 40,000 sq ft of storage space. Yet just three months later through his network he had closed six deals, which filled his warehouse and reaped business worth over £1.2m.

Marcus Emery succeeded because he understood that the true potential of any networking organisation lies not in the members themselves, but in the clients and contacts they hold. It is very easy upon your first visit to look out across your new networking group and see 20 – 40 "Customers", and to tailor your presentation from day one towards selling directly to the group. But to do so is to miss completely the purpose and potential of such a group. Big business comes to those with the vision to look beyond the room. Towards the end of the Empire, a new prison was built in British Columbia to replace the old Fort Alcan prison that for hundreds of years had housed the region's convicts. After the prisoners were moved into their new quarters, they were enlisted to dismantle the old buildings and spent long days stripping out the fixtures and plumbing, and then they came to the cells themselves, where they got a shock. For they found that indeed, there were huge locks attached to massive iron doors. There were even 2-inch bars on the windows. But the walls themselves were no more that paper and clay, painted to resemble iron. A mighty kick and they would have been through. For years they had been contained by little more than their own perception. Looking beyond the room with your network reveals what you actually buy into when you join a group: access to a well connected, active sales force for your business.

Indeed, whatever your size of company, when you join a modern networking group, you effectively become the sales director of a large company, with between 20 and 40 sales people at your disposal. And every presentation you give should be on that basis.

So what can you achieve in sixty seconds?

Here is an example presentation, from a businessman specialising in appealing local government taxation demands for companies.

"Good Morning, My name is John Smith and I am a rates consultant. Quite simply, I save you money on your business rates. If you are in business and paying rates, I may be able to appeal and reduce your costs. It will cost you nothing to find out, and my fees come from the money that you save. What sets me apart is the tremendous service that I give to my clients. No job is too small and no job too big. So if you or any of your business colleagues would like a free assessment, pass me a referral and I will be glad to help."

"John Smith – turning rates into rebates."

It looks good. John Smith has put together a great advert for his company. He has covered the key points of his business: he has emphasised the strength of the service he offers, the unlimited range of the rates demands he is prepared to take on, he has promoted himself to all – both directly to his network and to the clients and contacts they know. And finally, he has rounded it off with a memorable tag line – "John Smith – turning rates into rebates".

A great sounding presentation. But it is not one that will pull serious business

For there are 30 people in the room. Yes, your sales force want to help you, but yours is just one presentation among many. There is the distraction of a meal being served and the fact that many will be secretly working on their own presentation as you speak. The simple truth is that if you really want to choose your next customer, you have to make it easy for your sales force – and that means being brutally specific about the contacts you seek. There is a comfort in casting your net as wide as possible – to throw out the words "Anyone who, somebody who, everyone who…" as if your sales force was going to sit down, work out exactly who you intended and then go out and close them for you. But it is a cold comfort for your business. In networking, big business comes to those who show they know exactly what they want….and have the confidence to ask for it.

Two years ago, in a provincial town in the county of Kent, England, one of the members rose for her morning's presentation at the Tonbridge Chapter of BNI. Her name was Amanda Baker and she was a fine artist, who specialised in animal drawings and portraits. If ever there was an individual justified to ask for "anybody, somebody, everybody…." it was Amanda. But that is not what she did. Instead she had produced a superb drawing of a corgi dog, and as she held it up to the Chapter, she added, "Well you all know the referral that I want!!!" The Chapter laughed, and the meeting rolled on, seemingly as if nothing had happened. But Amanda Baker stopped laughing less than three hours later when she made a call that was answered "Buckingham Palace". She was requested to place her work before the Queen.

This is indeed a small world – but only when you get specific

Whenever I relay that story in seminars or trainings, there is usually a gasp of disbelief that such a thing should happen, but we really should not be so surprised. They say that you are never more than 5 people away from making contact with anyone in the world, and I have come to know that this is true. I recently gave a speech to 100 business people, in which I told a story about a contact I held in the Saudi Royal family. What surprised me was the people that approached me afterwards – each with a story of their own connection to Royal families in the UK, Spain, the Netherlands, and through the Middle East. Simply through the contacts in that room, I could have made contact with so many of the seemingly most private individuals in the world.

The truth is that this world becomes a very small place when you get specific. I learned this lesson very early on in my BNI career, when I found myself sitting next to one of my South of England members for a Christmas lunch. I had recently started setting up groups in the Midlands, and Alan Sutton asked me how the groups differ between those down South, where we were, and the new ones up North. A pleasant conversation ensued as I explained that the key difference was that up in the North they had members that actually produced things – manufacturers and engineers so rarely found in the South. But, then I got specific, and the world started to shrink. I started to tell Alan about a visitor that I had met. A man who produced vacuum pumps – huge room sized machines for use in heavy industry. I noticed Alan's face had changed and he was looking at me inquisitively. I paused, and he responded:

"This visitor. . . he wasn't by any chance a tall guy was he?"

"Yes", I replied.

"Had a beard?"

"Yes!"

"He's my brother-in-law!!"

I dug into my jacket pocket, and there was the business card of Alan's relation.

If being specific within a single group can give you access to Royalty throughout the world, and can find common ground between two people over a Christmas lunch, just imagine the power of working with a group of well connected local business people to draw contacts for your business into all of the regions companies you would choose. That is the potential of a focussed networking group, but one realised only by those who ask for exactly what they want. The clients you seek are probably paying the mortgages, holidays, school fees of the members who have them. Your network will pass them over, but only IF they understand just how important they are to you. For that to happen, you have got to identify clients you seek by name. An important contact into the British Royal family is not to be thrown around lightly. Amanda Baker could have been in her Chapter for a 1,000 years. She would never have received her dream referral, if she hadn't asked for it by name.

Being specific about the clients you seek extends far beyond the more obvious cases of "Dream" referrals – Royalty, Government contracts etc, to the everyday clients that form the bulk of your business. Recently in the U.K. the financial industry was turned on its head with the introduction of compulsory, "Stakeholder", pensions for all firms with 5 or more employees. At a stroke, a huge opportunity presented itself to every financial adviser, and for six months as I visited my BNI

◄◄

Take the time to ask yourself – Who do I want to do business with?

Chapters I heard the same presentation from each: "If you know any company with 5 or more employees that would be a great referral for me." Well of course, if we sat down and thought about it, we all knew many such firms and it might seem reasonable to expect a great avalanche of referrals flowing to the financial advisers in the weeks that followed. But nothing happened. Lost within 20-40 other such presentations, throwaway lines like "anybody, somebody, everybody" simply evaporate into the air. But again, it need not be that way.

Think back to the last time you bought a new car. You studied the brochures and pictured yourself behind the wheel. The visit to the showroom was an event - your chariot laid before you in all of its pristine glory. It was truly "your car" – it could have been the only one produced. Until the moment you handed over your money, left the forecourt, and drove out into the world – and suddenly it seemed everyone was driving them.

Of course, it was always thus – you just never had a reason to take notice before. Give your network a reason to take notice through brutally identifying example clients and customers, and referrals that were always there will scream out to your sales force.

Albert Einstein was once asked by a student, "How many inches are there in a mile?" Einstein's answer surprised the student for he said, "How should I know? Why should I fill my mind with such needless clutter that I can readily look up in a book?" We may not have minds quite so sharp as Einstein's, but our brains do work in very much the same way.

As you read this book now, you are filtering away all of the other distractions of your environment. The light, the ticking clock, the noise of the fridge in the kitchen. Of course, now I have drawn your attention to them, it is probably hard to get them out of your mind. When you identify by name companies you would seek to have as clients, what you are actually doing is building up a database in the minds of your network. If they can help you today, alarm bells will be ringing in their heads, but even if not, you have given them reason to take notice, and your database will sit securely in their minds, waiting for the day that they can.

And you do not often have to wait long

Most of us have had the experience in our lives where we have been chatting to a friend who mentioned a book, a song, or an individual that we are sure we have never heard of. But then, over the next week, we hear someone else mention it, our eyes are drawn to its mention in a newspaper, we spot a programme on just that subject on television. It was always there of course, but like Einstein, we had never had a reason to take notice before. Working your network is no different.

Last autumn, visiting one of our groups on the Sussex coast, I heard a member asking for an introduction to pharmaceutical companies. Had he left it there, no one would have taken notice and his plea would have fallen on deaf ears. But this member went further - he started giving names. In particular he wanted an introduction to Seton Healthcare, a company some 300 miles away in the North of the country. I was certain that I had never heard of Seton before, and he received no referrals that day. But a seed had been sown. It was just two months later, as I celebrated Christmas with my family, that I found my brother cursing his luck that he had to travel to Manchester straight after to visit an important client. Who was the client?

Seton Healthcare.

The key to drawing from any network the maximum benefit for your business, is always to know in advance **exactly** what you want from them. For some specialists – chiropractors, personal travel agents, and those who deal exclusively with personal clients, it is unrealistic to expect to be able, week on week, to name potential clients. Here you need to go a stage further – to focus upon those outside of your group who already refer business to you. Such **strategic alliances** underpin many businesses, and just one quality referral in this area can transform a company's fortunes.

I recently met up with one of our members in the health insurance industry. Each week he asked for individuals or companies seeking schemes and was having some success, but his presentations were about to change. As we discussed his business, I asked him how he found clients away from the group.

◀◀

Strategic Alliances offer perhaps the greatest networked potential of all

His answer was simple – the referrals from just two financial advisers formed the core of his company. A quality introduction to two more of course would practically double his operation. Unlike his clients, these people could be named, targeted, and at last his group could know exactly how to help him.

The Next Step

Being specific is the single most important element to a presentation designed to pull business. But, by itself it is not enough. For at the moment you recognise an opportunity to refer a colleague to one of your clients, you have a choice: You can take the plunge and start talking about your associates business. Or, more simply, you can quietly let the moment pass and an opportunity slip away. For your sales team to take that bold step with every client you seek, they are going to need a little more than just the names of your prospects – they are going to need both the confidence to refer you, and they are going to need to know what to say.

We do not run your business, and no matter how brave we like to think we are, most of us would

Remember, your network are looking to avoid the pain of cold calls

back away from an uncomfortable situation we don't need to face. Let my client down and my relationship with him will be damaged. Similarly, if he exposes my lack of knowledge about the person I am referring, my judgement elsewhere will also look flawed. Ask any member of a networking group what was the primary attraction of the group to them and most will answer: "The avoidance of cold calls!" But what is a cold call? A cold call is calling someone you don't know to talk about a business you do. That is not so far removed from speaking to a client you know well...about a business you don't.

I will never forget my first attempt to pass a quality third party referral to a member of my own Chapter. Sitting in front of a substantial client, the conversation unexpectedly turned to his on going marital difficulties, and in particular to his dissatisfaction with his lawyer. From nowhere, a referral for the solicitor in my group beckoned. I jumped straight in, speaking of him as if I'd known him for years, recommending his service with great passion. All was going well until my client through me the simplest curve – "That is great. Where is he based?!?"

It was some time before I felt the confidence to refer member's third party again!

The challenge with every presentation you give is to arm your sales force with all of the information they need to recommend you without hesitation whenever an opportunity presents itself. Thus it is not enough for John Smith to say "No job too big, no job too small". That is never true. If you want us to refer you we need to know for certain that this is a client you want. It is not enough to say: "What sets me apart is the tremendous service I give my clients". That is the claim of practically every one of us in business, and thus on its own, carries little weight. It would be a very special company indeed which, asked about its service, replied, "We don't really bother with that!"

If the members of your group are to refer you readily and with confidence, your presentation needs to be filled with specific stories of how you add value to your clients – interesting stories that your sales team will readily pass on to the prospects that you are seeking. Yet again, being specific makes it real to those that want to help you, and will spur them to action. Let's have a look at an alternative presentation for Mr Smith.

"Good Morning, My name is John Smith and I have just one aim – to save businesses money on their rates. This week, I have saved Soapy Sam's cleaning Company on Dean Street £2,000 from his rates bill. It cost Sam nothing to have his rates checked – my fee always comes from the savings that I make. Sam was so delighted that he has already referred me to his next-door neighbour. But I know that I could make similar savings for all of the companies on that road. So an introduction to Kall-Kwik Printers, The Curry Inn, or Jones Furnishings would be an ideal referral for me."

"John Smith on the High Street – turning rates into rebates."

Subtle changes to a presentation that make the world of difference in business

The changes are subtle, but the result is a presentation that will leave John Smith's network with all they need to refer him the business he is seeking. They know exactly whom he wishes to do business with this week; they will draw the confidence to refer him through the excellent work he has detailed with his delighted client, Soapy Sam; they know exactly what to say. Fellow members who know the companies mentioned, or any others on Dean Street will eagerly relay the message: "Did you know that Soapy Sam has just saved £2,000 on his rates bill. The person who enabled that for him was a close associate of mine, John Smith. **Would you like me to see if John can spare the time to have a look over your situation?"** Mr. Smith is heading for some very strong referrals indeed!

We began this section, looking at the temptation in any short presentation to attempt to cover every possible client, to ask for "anybody, somebody, everybody" but in fact, leave your sales force cold. One of the ironies of a specific, detailed presentation such as we have just seen, is that you actually open up your company to receive the "anybody, somebody, everybody" you were originally minded to ask for. Members of John's network, who know another cleaning company, will be sure to pass on the good news about Soapy Sam. And even if the members do not know any of the companies on Dean Street, they have precise examples of the type of companies he is seeking, and with the examples he has supplied, can take his message to those clients with security and confidence.

Armed with such presentations, referring fellow members switches from seeming a weekly burden into a joy. I once attended a network meeting in which a local banker was giving a presentation. Banks are great members in most networking organisations, but in the main, confine their presentations to seeking start-ups or businesses unhappy with their existing managers. Steve Tester, however, was different. He understood the need to clearly identify potential clients to his members, and then to tell them exactly what to say. As he rose to speak, he began by setting us a task – to take a look at the cheques passing daily through our companies. He explained that we would notice that many of them would be from local companies with banks seemingly far away. This occurred because the owners opened up a bank account when they were 17, left to go to University before relocating miles away from home and finally setting up in business. They had long since lost any personal contact with their bank. They could be a great referral for him.

Guide your network right through the referral process

At this point, Steve had opened up a potential stream of referrals for his bank, but he didn't leave it there. He led us through the referral process. He asked us to enquire, "Have you ever thought about switching to a more local bank?" He told us that we would receive the response "I've just never really got around to it", and then he told us what to say next: "Please do not say at this point "I know a good banker." I know that I am the banker for most of you in this room, what I would like you to say is "Can I introduce you to my banker?" This is personal, and I find it works every time."

It was just a few days later, concluding a sale in my art business, then a cheque came across my desk. As Steve had promised, the bank address was 100 miles away. Alarm bells rang in my head, and I fell into the conversation he had laid out so clearly. It was when I asked "Can I introduce you to my banker?" that I received my first reward. "Would you?" my client responded, "That is so kind." Helping Steve was bringing me closer to my client.

With a little preparation, and an understanding of the key factors behind a great presentation, the results can be dramatic and immediate. A few months ago, I found myself travelling with one of my assistants, David King, to a distant Chapter some 50 miles from his home base. David had never visited the Arundel chapter before, but decided that he wanted to represent his own business, mobile phones, that morning. So it was that, as we drove, a presentation started to form.

It turned out that David's company held the title of Cellnet (one of the major networks in the U.K.) Dealer of the Year for knowledge. By itself, this may not have been that exciting, but it became very useful for his presentation when he revealed two of the other title holders comprised perhaps the major players in the UK cellphone industry – "The Link" and "The Carphone Warehouse". So we crafted this information into his opening lines: "The Cellnet retailer of the year for group sales is The Link. The Cellnet dealer of the year for volume is The Carphone Warehouse. But the Cellnet dealer of the year for knowledge is the company that I own - Sussex Mobiles".

And thus he gave them the confidence to refer

Next, David worked in a superb story as to how he had served one of his clients – saving them time, and a great deal of money through his expertise.

Give us the confidence... tell us what to say... be brutally specific

He was telling them what to say

All we needed now was a specific "Call to action" – the name of a company in the area to ask for by name – no easy task at 6:00a.m. From our mobiles, we tried a National directory, and received several suggestions, but with no way to check their suitability, David was understandably reluctant to use them. As we pulled into Arundel, it was looking like we were going to be unlucky, but then, right in front of the venue, came the answer to our quest. Parked in the road stood a brand new van. From its appearance and quality sign writing, it was clear that it was both local and one of a fleet. Fleets all use mobile phones. The company was called A E Parker & Sons.

He was brutally specific about his target client

In truth, there were not many referrals passed that morning among the members. But one of them was to David King. Not for a one off, small, "Try you out" sale, but rather for the large company he had specifically requested – AE Parker & Sons.

Whenever and wherever you have the chance to present in public, keep in mind that such opportunities are a privilege, and one that rewards the focused. It is very tempting, particularly in a regular networking group to believe that if you get it wrong this week, there is always next week, or the week after. But weeks and months soon slip by, and bad habits die-hard. It is worth remembering that, given just one minute a week to speak on your business, you will have less than an hour a year to get your message across. And even if you remain in a networking group for your entire working life, you will speak for less than a single working week (40 hours) promoting your company to your sales force. There is no secret to effective presentations. Successful networkers naturally pursue the guidelines set out in this Chapter, and their success awaits all who follow this path.

Chapter Four

THE POWER OF TESTIMONY

It was handed over with the minimum of fuss and ceremony. The car dealer in the network rose to his feet and crossed the room towards the insurance agent. Few words were exchanged:

"This is the insurance for the Homebase vans", he commented.

"Thanks Alan", came the muted reply.

The referral round moved on, but my interest had been awakened. Homebase are a national chain of DIY stores in the U.K. and any referral there was likely to be substantial. I leant across to where Alan was seated. "Is that **The** Homebase?" I enquired.

"Yes", Alan responded, "Larry is to arrange the insurance on their vans."

I pressed on. "So, how many vans do Homebase operate?"

"600!"

Visit practically any modern referral based networking organisation and you will find a meeting comprised of two halves. For each member, the first half is very much about "Me, Me, Me!" For it is here that members educate their sales force on exactly how they can help them this week – with preparation, where they quite literally "Choose their next Customer". Indeed, one member will normally be offered 10 minutes or more to delve in some detail into his business, opening up his operation to the team that will assist him in finding new clients. It is a necessary, but essentially selfish, section that, in isolation contributes little to the building of relationships and trust.

But at a certain point, the meeting turns around, and from here on the emphasis is all about giving. It is at this moment that all top performers come alive. They know that in a networking environment every member is ALWAYS on show, and that they are being judged in everything they do. Givers do Gain. "Cop Out" here and no matter how great your presentation, a regular supply of high value, third party referrals will remain beyond your reach.

◄◄
Simply asking for business is not enough – you have got to be prepared to give

Some years ago, while seeking to strengthen their staff base of cabin crew, British Airways adopted a unique approach. Gathering together their pre-selected candidates into a single room, they challenged each in turn to take the platform in front, and present on their life history for two minutes. A daunting task for any of us, but a massive test for a group just leaving their teenage years, stepping out into the world for the very first time.

The results were disparate. Some stepped up and made a pretty good fist of it. They spoke quite confidently and eloquently, and returned to their seats full of confidence that the job was in the bag. Others stuttered and stumbled, a few even drying up completely, and returned to their seats deflated, just as certain that an opportunity had passed them by.

But British Airways had a twist. For the job on offer was not public speaking but the welfare of passengers. And the assessors paid no mind to those on the stage. They were looking solely out to the audience. Those that offered encouragement to the candidates struggling up front, applauding efforts no matter how successful, were set to become an air steward. They would be the ones who, at 40,000 feet, would offer you or me a blanket if they thought we were cold. Those that remained silent, perhaps working on their own presentation, or basking in the success of their particular speech, were in reality standing by as their hoped for career ebbed away.

As you stand to speak at the second half of a networking meeting, all eyes are upon you. And just as with British Airways, the rewards are ultimately reaped by those who, yes, seek to give business, but even beyond that, who show real appreciation for the people who make up their sales team. And that means giving powerful, prepared testimonies. It is very tempting to view testimonials as a quick sidestep – a convenient cover for those barren meetings where you have no business to pass. But to do so is to let slip one of the most powerful tools in the networkers armoury – Recognition. One of our Assistant Directors in BNI, Ray Finn sums it up beautifully: "Soldiers die for it, babies cry for it." Say thank you to me and that is good – I appreciate it, but the feeling is momentary, lost almost as the next speaker rises to

◄◄

"Soldiers Die for it,
Babies cry for it." –
Recognition

his feet. But deliver a powerful, carefully worded testimonial that touches my heart, that confirms to the members present the calibre of my business – and you will have me seeking business for you for the next year.

As ever, there is no short cut to such a presentation – you have got to be prepared. Picture the scene. You have taken a risk with your reputation. You have referred a member to one of your best clients. They have come through – the feedback from your client has been superb. Give again now, and not only will you reinforce the goodwill of the recipient, but more than that, your entire network will be motivated to seek work for you. By the time you sit down every single member of the group should be wishing they had been the one receiving your praise.

But the job is still not done. Emotions are short lived and memories will soon fade. To secure lasting impact you need to go further, you need to **write it down**. Step into a taxi in the centre of Kuala Lumpur, and the feeling is very much the same as with any modern metropolis. A mass of identical vehicles with seemingly nothing to choose between them. It is strange then, that upon landing in KL, my first act is always to seek out just one driver.

I remember very well the first time I met Jensen. He was waiting outside the Shangri-La Hotel in the standard battered, old, Proton Saga that forms the staple for taxi drivers there. It was when I got in that my experience changed. As we dropped onto the first set of traffic lights, he turned to me and said, "Would you like to see my book sir?" I opened it, and found myself working through page after page of written testimonies to Jensen's driving. From all over the world, businessmen, tourists and locals testified to his reliability. I could rest easy – I knew I was in good hands, and from that day on when I have an important engagement there is only one man who will get the business.

A carefully worded written testimonial affords the recipient a powerful, third party "Referred" backing to every business deal they seek. And, as so often in life, the benefits flow back to their source. If you are wondering why a member of your network has not referred you to his clients, why not give him a reason to speak of you to all of his customers and prospects – through a powerful written testimonial **on your letterhead**.

Today, Jensen's book carries an additional message – this time from Andrew Hall at BNI, complete with my email and phone number, just in case any KL business travellers would like to get in touch.

Chapter Five

THE COMPLETE NETWORKER

I remember the arrival of John Adams very well. From the moment he joined forces with his group in Sussex, it was as if a jolt of electricity had shot through the Chapter. Activity levels soared, referrals boomed. What started as a trickle of referrals to him became a steady stream, and then a raging torrent. Just six months into his membership, he had closed £400,000 in business through the group. Less than a year later, the figure approached £2million. £2million in closed business through a myriad of referred opportunities passed by a chapter of just 30 quality business entrepreneurs.

3 months later, he was gone. That seemingly unstoppable flow of business had dried, and he had nowhere left to turn.

He is not alone.

To a new member, great presentations offer the fastest route to high-level third party business. But the complete networker knows only too well that this is just the beginning. For it is how you respond to the opportunities passed your way, and the trust that you build with your sales force that will prove the final arbiter of your success.

◀◀

A referral received is only the beginning

Think back for a moment to the start of your business career, and the day you received your very first referral. Suddenly, you had a hot lead. Someone was in the market for your product or services, and more than that, they were waiting for your call. Nervous with anticipation, you jumped straight onto the phone. You chased it down as if it was closed business. And of course, it did close.

The next time you had such a feeling of true anticipation from a referred opportunity was probably the first referral passed to you by your network. A recommended opportunity handed over on a small slip of paper. Again, you locked on to it like an exocet. Again it closed. But in the months and years that follow, many pieces of paper flow across that table, some strong, some not so. Good or bad, they all look the same, all passed on small slips of anonymous paper. It is all too easy to begin to pre-judge. Indeed, as your ambitions rise and you begin to ask for larger and larger introductions, almost out of necessity, the quality of the referrals seems to weaken. Ask for an introduction to the printer in your town and someone will know him well. Ask for the Managing Director of a pharmaceutical giant thirty miles away, and members may know a secretary, or a manager in the wrong department.

For so many ex-members of network organisations, the demise of their membership can be traced to the day they first started to "Take a view" on the paper they were passed. The burden of that wasted trip, that embarrassed phone call to a "Referral" who had not heard of you, hangs heavy, and it is all too easy to lose sight of the potential in today's recommendations. Newspaper tycoon Robert Maxwell became increasingly defensive as his complex web of businesses started to unwind. Threatening and aggressive letters invaded his mail to the point where he forbade his staff from opening any letter addressed personally to him. Weeks passed and the mail continued to pile up around his office. Finally, one member of staff resolved to come in and go through it all over the weekend, piece by piece. There among the writs and the accusations, was a cheque for £1million.

The key to continued success in referral marketing is to treat every succeeding referral as if it was that first one. For a member is watching you. "Take a view", dismiss the opportunity he has passed, and you can be sure he will not pass another. But treat it with respect, chase it down like it was closed business, thank him for his effort, and he will go on to seek out more referrals, high quality opportunities for a colleague he can trust.

⏮ *Treat every referral as if it were your first*

Indeed, as with so much in life, what you get is in no short part determined by where you place your own expectation. National newspapers today exchange hands for huge sums because the magnates know the practical impossibility of launching a new paper into an already saturated market. So it is somewhat surprising that USA Today should have risen from nothing to dominate the news-stands in America in just twenty years. Even more impressive to find that the launch of this unknown paper in 1982 was attended by perhaps the most important figures in America at the time – Ronald and Nancy Reagan, Tip O'Neil, the speaker of the House of Representatives, Howard Baker, the Leader of the Senate. Almost unbelievable when you consider all of this was put together by an ex country boy from South Dakota, Al Neuharth. But Neuharth is a man whose expectation, when placed in front of any opportunity, is one of total success. Asked how he attracted so many of the great and the good to kick off his paper, his answer was a simple one – "I asked them!"

Consistent networkers carry this conviction throughout their working lives – they chase every referral as if it was closed business. Two years ago, as I sat in my office in Sussex, the phone rang and I found myself talking to a man with a real purpose.

His business was the sale of Jumbo Jets – huge airliners fitted out for the Super-rich and Royal families of the world, and retailing in excess of $40m. Come to a networking event and ask for "Anyone who wants a $40m jet!" and you will surely draw a blank. But that is what made this man so interesting, and over the next few months, he was to teach me a great deal about the commitment and dedication exhibited by top networkers.

He had isolated his clients down tightly for his network, and in so doing he had been referred to me. On the face of it, a very weak referral – I had no reason to help him at all. All he knew was that one of my clients **was** in the market for the kind of planes in which he dealt. But I felt no connection with him and as I put down the phone, paid little mind to his request. My indifference ceased a couple of hours later, however, when a motorcycle courier pulled up outside the office and handed me a package. Inside I discovered a complete dossier on this man's company and the plane in question. There was the company history, his own background (I noticed we had gone to the same university and suddenly felt a bond), there were full details on the plane in – its lifetime log and service history, complete with a CD Rom giving information on every inch of its layout.

Here was a man giving me the confidence to refer him, and what is more, he was telling me what I should say.

The eight months that followed proved to be the busiest of my life thus far and if I am honest, I would quite willingly have dropped the project at any time. But every couple of weeks the phone would ring, an email would arrive, a fax would be sent – a gentle reminder, a polite enquiry if he could help me with any more information. He just never gave up. And like so many people who just never give up, at the end of those eight months, he reaped his reward when I finally secured the appointment with the Royal contact he was seeking.

Whether your market is Jumbo Jets or paperclips, the fundamentals of networking remain the same. Treat every opportunity as if it is closed business. Recently, I met a member of my networking organisation in the Midlands, who approached me excitedly because he had just closed a large piece of business. His company installed data cabling and the contract was worth £125,000. He had done it exactly the right way – he had named the client he wished to secure, and on the day he did so, he picked up 4 referrals. But as the dust settled and he looked over his crop of paper, his heart sank. Asking for the Managing Director of this company, he had instead received referrals to a secretary to the finance director, the cleaner of the offices, a security guard – nobody remotely at the level he needed. He had a choice – to "Take a view" and let it pass, or he could chase them down like they were closed business. He took the latter. He called the security guard, the cleaner and the secretary, got to know them and asked if they would be kind enough to see if they could help him. A short while after, he found himself invited to meet with the Managing Director. But the biggest surprise was yet to come. For as he entered the room, the boss came bounding round his desk to greet him and said, "I am so pleased to meet you. I have heard so much about you."

You never know who holds an influence in the large firms you may seek. As so often in life, the things you aspire to grow from the unlikeliest seeds, and then

You never know who holds an influence in the companies you seek

only if cared and nurtured along the way. Churchill's aunt once warned a man applying for the job of Winston's private secretary to "Remember, you will see all of Winston's faults in the first five hours. It will take you a lifetime to discover his virtues." For the cleaner in that Midland's firm, it may have been the first time he had had the opportunity to help anyone. Suddenly, he was important. For perhaps the first time, he could make a difference. He alone had the power to help this fellow human being. He probably chased it down like it was closed business – and so should you!

Chapter Six

GIVE AND YOU WILL RECEIVE

Step away from a modern referral based networking meeting and, on the face of it, you have little to show for the mornings effort. There will be the cards of the visitors that morning – both a source of business and a future resource for your company. There will be the referrals you have received – simple slips of paper filled with potential. And that is it.

Or is it? For dig deeper and there is something else. In all likelihood, you will have given referrals. Worked correctly, referrals passed can impact your business just as surely as referrals received.

I well remember my early days as a member of one of the first focussed networking organisations in the UK. The receipt of a referral would be the signal for a massive effort to ensure its closure. But as I gave them out, I very much left it to the recipient to take on the challenge from there. If they needed help, they would surely call.

I was making a mistake...

One on One meetings – the foundation stone behind every successful networker

One on Ones – meeting a fellow member of your network away from the usual forum – offers, perhaps the most effective opportunity for dramatic new business to the active networker, particularly where held between members with seemingly little in common. It is all too easy to concentrate on those with whom you have a natural synergy – the accountant with the solicitor, the builder with the plumber and decorator – and thereby miss out on the massive possibilities that lie elsewhere. For you never know from where the next large-scale referral will come. Recently, in Berkshire England, a BNI member asked for an introduction to the Managing Director of Motorola, a high-tech company with a heavy interest in the area. His request was answered, but not as you may think, by one of the many professionals in the room – the banker, solicitor, or the IT specialist. It came from the decorator, part way through a project in the Managing Director's home.

Such opportunities arise where business people seek out the possibilities through their entire network – through meeting one-on-one. For it is only when two people get together face to face that misunderstandings, pre-conceptions, and doubts clear away, replaced, in turn, by a clear strategy and a willingness to help.

At the height of the Iranian crisis in 1979, anti American and anti British demonstrations had become part of daily life, and Tehran did not appear a very healthy place to be for a Western face. But amazing things happen when you meet one on one, and the reporters there soon discovered something quite different. BBC reporter John Simpson speaks of a time when he faced a seething mob in Tehran, all baying for Western blood. "Death to England, Death to Thatcher" raged the crowd. One man in particular became so intense that froth spilled from his mouth as he roared his chant. With nowhere to run, Simpson faced the man, and somewhat unwisely announced: "Hello, I am from England. I work for the B.B.C." The reaction was immediate. The old man calmed, took his hand, kissed it and replied, "You are very welcome in Iran. I hope that you like our country."

We may not need to engineer quite the change in attitude that Simpson achieved, yet the benefits from turning member acquaintances into solid business allies, through showing an interest in their businesses with one on one meetings, is a prize that most members still evade.

Nestled among the members of my own BNI group in Kent were two business people who had studiously avoided seeking a close relationship. Graham Adams was a financial adviser and knew that Denise, while a great business lady and estate agent, had a financial services arm to her business and therefore, surely, she would never refer him. It was two years before they finally met, one-on-one, although not by choice, but forced in a random draw held by the Chapter Director. Reluctantly, they agreed to meet. Two hours later, and business opportunities worth in excess of £150,000 had been settled, as the two "Competitors" discovered ways to work together for mutual advantage.

When considering with whom in your chapter to have a meeting, it is logical and right that you should start with those who have just referred you. Having your referrer work closely in helping you chase down his opportunity is an aid too good to miss. But, if ever there was an individual to have a one-on-one with, it is the person to whom you have just **referred** an opportunity. Most obviously, this member owes you, and will be eager to repay your contribution. "Givers' Gain" works because people work to refer those that have in turn referred them. But of more immediate significance, here is someone about to step foot inside the door of one of YOUR clients. If there is one thing that is guaranteed in a referral situation, it is that the client and the referred member will talk about the person who brought them together. Send him in blind, and anything he mentions about you or your business could do damage. But prime him, tell him what to say and perhaps, for the very first time, you will have an "Unbiased" advocate for your

⏮

If ever there was a person to have a One on One meeting with, it is the person you have just referred

business, inside your client company, opening doors in a way that only those with "No Axe to Grind" can.

At the heart of the success of referral organisations, lies the observation that people latch on and take note of third party recommendations, just as surely as they reject direct sales. The forces that led my Royal contact to grant an audience to someone marketing a jet plane, were no different from those that made the boss of a large company take a recommendation for a data cabler from his cleaner. There is a security and confidence around recommendations made by a third party. Use it wherever you are referring a business to one of your clients, and you will not only reinforce your relationship with that client, you will open up opportunities for new business that you could never achieve on your own.

Joining BNI in 1997, I was running a business providing mobile phones and telecom solutions to the corporate market. New out at that time was a device that combined mobile technology with the GPS system. It allowed the fleet owners of cars, vans and lorries to see exactly where their vehicles were, and more interestingly – where they had been. The early results were impressive – most owners found that productivity increased and fraud fell away as they introduced the devices. Convinced of the benefit, I pressed its case to a distribution company I held as a client. I sent them information and costings, pitched directly to the Managing Director, but all to no avail. Typical of brand new technology, the units were expensive then and I could not break the feeling that I would gain more than the company! Until, that is, I referred one of my fellow members into the firm. Just two days later, the MD of the distribution company gave me a call.

"Could you come over and show us your system again. We would like a second look."

The product had not changed, the message had not changed, but the carrier of the message had. For the first time I had an ally with no direct connection to my business, able to refer my company back to the very client I had introduced him to. Simple and effective, one-on-one meetings, with all of those to whom you refer third party, open the potential for new business from perhaps your best prospects of all – the clients you already have.

Chapter Seven

REFERRAL MAGIC!!! QUALITY BUSINESS CONJURED OUT OF THIN AIR!

Givers' Gain – If I give Business to You, You Will Want to Give Business Back to Me - the founding philosophy of the referral network organisation, Business Network International.

Look over the shelves of any supermarket or grocery store today, and there, on the back of almost any packet, tin, or box, will be a coupon. Simple promotions – send in three coupons with a little postage and packing, and the manufacturer will forward the latest gift. Those that do, send their replies not directly to the producer, but to mail forwarders – specialist companies that handle promotions and mailings, thereby removing the burden from the manufacturer.

Chris Peck ran just such a business, "Mastermail", from his base in the heart of Sussex. For some time, he had watched enviously as the considerable coupon business of Cadbury's mashed "potato" product, "Smash" landed not at his door, but passed to one of his competitors. Chris had done his homework. The man he needed to speak to was Michael Knight. He had already tried to call him without success, he had sent faxes and emailed, without response. Finally, he turned to his Chapter.

Given just one minute to present his case each week, Chris asked directly for an introduction to Michael Knight.

Nothing Happened!

Cadbury's business was based some 200 miles away and no one in the group had contacts there. Several weeks later, Chris asked again.

Nothing Happened!

◄◄

Sometimes, you need to ask more than once

Finally, Chris decided to give it one more try. He explained to the group the importance of this client, how he had faxed, phoned and emailed without effect. He really needed an introduction.

Nothing Happened! Nothing that is, except one member picked up the phone, and made a call. It was 4:30 on a Sunday afternoon when Chris Peck's home phone rang. A stranger's voice on the other end of the line introduced himself: "This is Michael Knight. I hear that you want to speak with me!"

Underpinning the philosophy of "Givers' Gain" is the notion that people do not just want to help people; they want to help those who in turn are giving individuals. What drove me to refer my biggest client to a man selling 747's whom I had never heard of before; what led a cleaner to take the trouble to recommend a data cable specialist, whom he scarcely knew, to his boss at work, was the same force that persuaded Michael Knight to pick up the phone. For the member who made the call to Cadbury's had a unique approach. Anyone who has ever cold called for his or her own gain knows that the experience can be a bruising one.

The recipient is immediately on his guard and, by instinct, becomes determined to get rid of the caller at the earliest moment. But make a call simply to help a fellow man, and the rules change. When Gail Williams picked up the telephone, she was not seeking to help herself – she was helping a friend with a need.

It is human nature to want to help those who in turn seek only to help others

"I have a problem, and only you can help me", she opened to the secretary charged with "fielding" Mr Knight's calls. She explained that she was a member of a quality referral organisation and a member, held in high regard, had repeatedly asked for an introduction to Michael Knight. It was clear that no one in the group had any contacts with Cadbury's. Could she arrange for Michael to give Chris a call?

On hearing this story, it is very tempting to dismiss it, to put it down to "Beginners Luck" and ignore the potential it reveals. But it was picked up by one of my Assistant Directors, David King, who started to put it to the test. Gathering about him requests from quality members who had repeatedly made specific requests to firms unknown to the members of their groups, he started making calls. "I have a problem, and only you can help me..." Suddenly, a financial adviser found himself pitching for the business of one of the largest print firms in the South; a video producer was placed in direct contact with the school he had often requested; a stationery supplier was placed in front of No.7 Labs – his target client ready to hear him. Into his tenth call and he was enjoying himself.

One of the core strengths of networking is that, by nature we are all more comfortable saying "He is great", than pushing our own cause. By the time David had finished making his calls, his success rate ran at over 80%. People want to help those who in turn help others. Carry this with you, and no door will ever be firmly closed to the members of your network.

With the knowledge that it is within your grasp to open the door to almost any company targeted by your network, the true potential of focussed networking for the modern business person is finally revealed. The limitations to success are found only in the strength of your relationships with your fellow members. Like everything in life, nothing is achieved without effort. This is Net-WORK! But the ability to work with a group of non competing business people; to be able to identify exactly who you want to do business with, and then have your network bring those customers primed to your door, is a prize worth working for. Focus on every aspect of your relationships with your network – your attendance, commitment, contribution, follow up, testimonies, and support, and you will build a network that will take your business wherever your ambition desires.

BIBLIOGRAPHY

Part I: Networking Fundamentals by Robert French

Brian Tracey "The Psychology of Achievement" (tape)

Dale Carnegie "How to Win Friends and Influence People" (Vermilion)

Napoleon Hill "Think and Grow Rich" (Wilshire Book Company)

Zig Ziglar "Goals" (Nightingale-Conant)

Anthony Robbins "Unleash the Power Within" (Simon & Schuster)

Robert Kiyosaki "Rich Dad,Poor Dad" "The Cashflow Quadrant" (Tech Press Inc)

Part II: The Complete Networker by Andrew Hall

Muhammad Ali "The Greatest", (Ballantine Press)

Mick Brown "Richard Branson – The Inside Story", (Michael Joseph).

John Charmley "Churchill – The End of Glory", (Hodder & Stoughton)

Maurice Corina "Pile it High, Sell it Cheap", (Weidenfeld & Nicolson)

Multiple Authors "Churchill by his Contemporaries", (Observer Books)

Edwards / Douglas "Getting Business to Come to You" (Tarcher Putnam)

Alison Fendley "Saatchi & Saatchi – The Inside Story", (Arcade)

Thomas Hauser "Muhammad Ali", (PAN)

James Humes "The Wit and Wisdom of Winston Churchill", (Harper Perennial)

Krass "The Book of Entrepreneurs Wisdom", (Wiley Publishing)

Ivan Misner "Worlds Best Known Marketing Secret", (Bard Press)

Misner / Davis "Business by Referral", (Bard Press)

David Thomas "Alan Sugar: The Amstrad Story", (Trafalgar Square)